COME WIND COME WEATHER

BUNYAN'S PILGRIM IN TODAY'S WORLD

John H Taylor

Jointly published 1987 by

The United Reformed Church in the United Kingdom
86 Tavistock Place
London WC1H 9RT

and

The Baptist Union of Great Britain and Ireland
4 Southampton Row
London WC1B 4AB

ACKNOWLEDGEMENTS:

Unless otherwise noted the Scripture quotations contained herein are from the *Revised Standard Version* of the Bible, copyrighted 1946, 1952 and 1971 by the Division of Education of the National Council of the Churches of Christ in the USA and are used by permission. All rights reserved.

Quotations from *Markings* by Dag Hammarskjøld (translated by W H Auden and Leif Sjøberg): © 1964 Reprinted by permission of Faber & Faber Ltd.

The quotation from *The Right to Believe:* © 1986 Keston College, reprinted with permission.

The quotation from *Window on my Heart* by Lady Baden-Powell: © 1983 The Girl Guides Association, reprinted with permission.

Cover by Neil Pinchbeck
Maps by Lewis Orchard

Typeset and Printed by Tyndale Press (Lowestoft) Ltd.

ISBN 0-902256-82-3.

CONTENTS

ACKNOWLEDGEMENTS

Without the encouragement and generosity of many people this little book would never have appeared. A great debt of thanks is due to those responsible for publishing in the United Reformed Church and the Baptist Union, in particular to Alma Wade, Carol Rogers, Norman Hart, Roger Spiller and Douglas Sparkes. Cyril Franks, Kenneth Wadsworth, Bill Hancock and Kenneth Slack made valued comments on the text. Terry Oakley and Donald Black helped with the questions.

Facilities were provided by Dr Williams's Library and Spurgeon's College.

Dr N H Keeble and the Oxford University Press have been generous in allowing their text to be used.

A sabbatical was made possible by the kindness of the URC Ministries Department, the Southern Provincial Synod and Beckenham United Reformed Church. It was made enjoyable by the staff of the Windermere Centre.

Throughout I have had the encouragement of my wife, Betty.

JOHN H TAYLOR

FOREWORDS

How appropriate it is that the United Reformed Church and the Baptist Union should jointly publish this book to commemorate the 300th anniversary of John Bunyan's death. He belonged to the early history of us both.

The seventeenth century was a rich biblical age. First came the publication of the Authorised Version of the Bible. Then came a succession of spiritual giants who made the Bible live in the faith and experience of many people — Richard Baxter, John Milton, George Herbert, George Fox and John Bunyan.

Bunyan was a skilled interpreter and communicator of scripture. His *Pilgrim's Progress* became a classic of English literature and Christian devotion. He wrote it with the sort of inspired imagination, evangelical passion and penetrating insight into the human situation which we sorely need in our generation.

This book by John Taylor is not a nostalgic journey back to Bunyan's days but a helpful retracing of the essential spiritual pilgrimage in the context of life in today's world. May it help those who read it to grasp what Bunyan said he 'smartingly did feel'.

Bernard Green
General Secretary,
The Baptist Union of Great Britain and Ireland.

We have two great English classics about pilgrims — Chaucer and Bunyan. Chaucer gives us the scenery of human society through the mouths of his pilgrim party, and human interest is the priority. Bunyan looks at life through the glass of faith. All the travellers are seen as participants in the greater pilgrimage which is through this visible life to the presence of God. Going to Canterbury was simple compared with the journey from here to God.

We know it. All the dangerous attractions and sorrows trap us, our eyes wander, we ask if it is all mirage and we sometimes get tired. So we need the vision of this brave pilgrim to remind us of the eternal country to which we travel and the inexhaustible riches of love and truth which feed us on the way.

We are grateful for this reflection on Bunyan's enduring work, making it readily accessible, contemporary, nourishing. It is an ideal study for Lent, and our thanks go to John Taylor as our guide and to the tinker himself who speaks with the true accents of a wayfaring man.

Bernard G Thorogood
General Secretary,
The United Reformed Church in the United Kingdom.

INTRODUCTION

1988 being the tercentenary of John Bunyan's death, it seemed right to honour his memory by blowing the dust off his famous allegory, *The Pilgrim's Progress,* and inviting Christians to think about some of the events and characters in it with a view to seeing their permanent spiritual value, and Lent seemed a good time to do it.

The book, then, is set out in 47 sections, one for each day of Lent, plus the days leading up to Easter Day. It could be used in the Lent of any year, or indeed at a time other than Lent. Ideally a reader should take one section every day, together with its question for the individual, but it is not essential. Seven sections might be read once a week, though mental and spiritual digestion might suffer.

For the sake of those without a copy of the allegory to hand I have tried to say enough in each section to make sense. Furthermore, a diagrammatic map is provided to help people find their way to any part of the work, whatever their edition may be. Page references in this book apply to the Oxford University Press *The World's Classics* series edition prepared by N H Keeble. The quotations preserve the seventeenth-century spellings and italics.

Prudence whispers that one should be sure to tell readers what this book is not about. It is not a commentary on the allegory, nor is it about Bunyan's life and times. It avoids the intricacies of seventeenth-century theology, which would prove bewildering, not to say boring, as a Lent study. It is no scholarly book. It is not a guide to spirituality. What, then, is it? Simply an attempt to draw from Bunyan's tale stimuli for reflection, self-examination and prayer.

Questions for group work are also appended, but please provide your own as well. There is nothing like talking to one another and facing common problems to deepen spiritual life and comfort pilgrims.

The materialism and secularism of our times have led to a healthy reaction, namely to a revival of interest in the life of the spirit. It is a shame, though, that not more use has been made of the spiritual treasures in the nonconformist tradition. The immense resources of the Catholic tradition are invaluable but suffer from one disadvantage, if not two. They come from spiritual directors used to living in religious communities; they tend to make the rest of us feel like second-class Christians. Furthermore, they generally belong to the cultured end of town.

Bunyan provides a balance. He is working-class, a tinker till he became a pastor; he shares with Amos a deep suspicion of the upper-classes. He writes of Christian and Christiana, ordinary followers of Christ, belonging to a community, a local church, but passing most of their time in the world. In our day they would be driving to work through dense traffic every morning, strolling together in the supermarket, getting up in the night to attend to a crying child. Such Christians in Bunyan's time were proud to call themselves 'saints' yet, as Keeble says, they seem 'improbable saints and unlikely heroes for a story'. This, however, is the very point of the allegory.[1]

The Pilgrim's Progress was written in two parts at widely different times. Part II, about Christian's wife and friends' pilgrimage, is reckoned to be the poor relation of Part I, and there is no denying this. Consequently, most of our study is to do with Part I, but some sections come from II and there is some cross-referencing. Part I is quasi-autobiographical. Part II hasn't its intensity; it is mellowed, having been distilled by a careful and loving pastor.

Now it seems to me pedantic to keep on saying *The Pilgrim's Progress,* which is the proper title. It has become common, and it seems easier to the tongue, to say *Pilgrim's Progress,* and I hope I may be excused for so doing.

1 *The Pilgrim's Progress*, p xvii.

ABBREVIATION

PP *Pilgrim's Progress, OUP The World's Classics series*, edited and introduced by N H Keeble (1984)

Come Wind, Come Weather
Actually Survey'd and
Delineated - March 1987
by Lewis Orchard Esq.
Lewes E. Sussex
City of Destruction
Evangelist
1–5.
Pliable
Slough of Despond – 6.
Worldly Wiseman
Evangelist
Road to Morality
7.
8. Wicket Gate

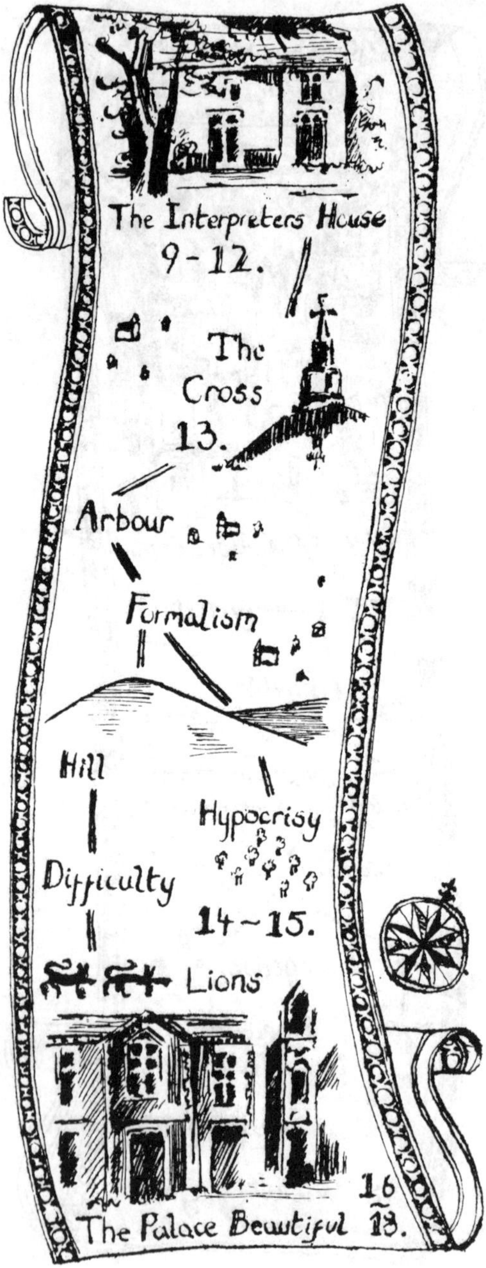
The Interpreters House
9-12.
The Cross
13.
Arbour
Formalism
Hill
Difficulty
Hypocrisy
14-15.
Lions
The Palace Beautiful
16
18.

Valley of
Humiliation.
19.
Apollyon.
20.
Valley of
21. the Shadow of Death.
22-24.
Faithful.
Inn.
39-42.

Talkative.
25~27.
WHITE H HOTEL
28~29. Vanity Fair.
30. By-ends.
31. Hopeful.
Doubting Castle.
32.
33~36.
43. Delectable Mts.
Mr Great-Heart.
37-38.
Mount Zion
47.
River of Death.
44-45.
N

SOME DATES

Heavy type refers to national history.
Other dates refer to John Bunyan.

1625	**Charles I becomes King**
1628	Birth at Elstow, Bedford
1640	**Long Parliament**
1642-6	**Civil War**
1643	**Westminster Assembly first meets**
1645-7	Soldier in Parliamentary Army
1648/9?	First marriage (four children)
1653	**Cromwell becomes Lord Protector**
1654	Joins Gifford's church
1656	Begins preaching
1658	Death of first wife
1659	Second marriage to Elizabeth (three children)
1660	**The Restoration — Charles II**
1660	Arrested and imprisoned for preaching at a Conventicle
1662	**The Great Ejectment from livings of those who will not conform to the Prayer Book**
1672	Pastor of Bedford church; released from gaol
1677	In prison six months
1678	*Pilgrim's Progress* published; written during long imprisonment
1682	*Second Part of Pilgrim's Progress*
1688	Death, 31 August; buried at Bunhill Fields on 3 September

1. THE DREAM

Pilgrimage

Lent is a time for reflection on life, for penitence, resolution and thanksgiving. At first sight it may seem strange to associate it with *Pilgrim's Progress* since John Bunyan belonged to a dissenting church which kept neither Good Friday nor Easter, let alone Lent. That we can do so is due to the reconciling and healing work which the Holy Spirit has inspired in modern times between Christians of different traditions. In *Pilgrim's Progress* we have the reflections of a Christian on life, with its ups and downs, its joys and sorrows, its moods, fears, choices and encounters.

Keeping Lent is of great antiquity. Leo the Great, Bishop of Rome, 440-461, preached about it. Points he made about spiritual combat, putting on Christian armour, overcoming the tempter, exposing pride and hypocrisy, growing in faith and goodness, and practising forgiveness and reconciliation, are allegorised in *Pilgrim's Progress.* Are they not part and parcel of Christian living whatever our age, culture or denominational home?

Pilgrim's Progress purports to be a dream.

> As I walked through the wilderness of this world, I lighted on a certain place, where was a Denn; And I laid me down in that place to sleep: And as I slept I dreamed a Dream.[1]

The den was Bedford gaol. The same isolation and irksome restriction which drove men like the Apostle Paul and the German pastor Bonhöffer to write letters, caused Bunyan to cultivate his own gift for writing. Perhaps the dream was something of a relaxation for him after writing the more conventional, though impassioned, autobiographical *Grace Abounding to the Chief of Sinners.* It allowed him to expose his lively imagination; indeed, to write an early precursor of the English novel.

The dream format has great importance for us, who are seeking out the spiritual significance of *Pilgrim's Progress,* for in a dream we throw aside normal constraints. Again and again in our study we shall see how the dreamer casts away his contemporary Puritan garb and reveals himself as a Christian of any age.

A book with life's forward movement as its theme is almost bound to take the journey or pilgrimage as its backbone. Pilgrimage has, of course, a long history.

Did not our Lord enter Jerusalem in triumph at the end of a pilgrimage? And people are still setting off for Lourdes or Rome. Visits to Iona and Taizé are also very much like pilgrimages. A pilgrimage provides plenty of excitement, with strange sights, interesting encounters, memorable adventures, usually in very good company. This can be true of any holiday. How people love to talk about where they plan to go on holiday, and when they come back home, to relate their adventures. It is sad that everyday life should be so lacking in interest or so forbidding that a few weeks' holiday each year becomes the staple diet of so much conversation. Bunyan, who never strayed far from Bedford, certainly not out of the Home Counties, is telling us in this book that the life of adventure and excitement is just where we are and live day by day.

Olive Wyon mentions in *On the Way* how Keats once said that our life is a 'perpetual allegory', everything in it only having meaning as it points to something beyond.[2] The Holy Grail, after which medieval knights were sent questing, had the same purpose: to return home with a fresh vision of life's significance. Throughout our study we shall be implicitly asking whether life is only a journey from the cradle to the grave, or a pilgrimage to 'the city with firm foundations, whose architect and builder is God'.[3]

1. PP p 8.
2. *Op cit* p 19.
3. Hebrews 11:10.

2. WHAT SHALL I DO?

Crisis

> I dreamed, and behold *I saw a Man, clothed with Raggs standing in a certain place, with his face from his own House, a book in his hand, and a great burden upon his Back.* I looked and saw him open the Book, and read therein; and not being able longer to contain, he brake out with a lamentable cry; saying, *what shall I do?*[1]

What brought about this crisis? It was a sombre convergence of internal and external problems, of personal and social pressures.

Returning to his house, he was obliged to give some explanation of his melancholy to his family. He told them little about himself, but elaborated on the subject of the state of the world. 'Our city will be burned with fire from heaven,' he warned, but nobody took him seriously.

Bunyan's relish for comedy takes over at this point. His 'sore amazed' relatives packed the man off to bed, 'hoping that sleep might settle his brains,' but it did not, so they resorted to getting angry with him, then to deriding him and chiding him, finally to neglecting him, all to no avail.

'What shall I do to be saved?' Overshadowed by the threat of a nuclear Armageddon, this is a question the world now asks itself. If Bunyan found his times bad, the vision of the Commonwealth having turned into a nightmare from which the nation was glad to awake, what shall we say of our times? There is no need to weary the reader with a list of our ills, national and international, for they are on everyone's lips.

But perhaps one victim ought to be mentioned, not forgotten. Isn't love becoming an endangered species? Readers will think immediately of casualties known to them in the field of domestic life. If, however, we turn to Alvin Toffler's *Future Shock,* which was compulsory reading for President Nixon's cabinet, we find love as we know it doomed. Morris West in his novel *Harlequin* dwells on the same theme.

George Harlequin, a Swiss high-flyer, leaves his wife because, in the words of his wife Julia, 'he's stepped into this new world where there is no love at all'.[2]

How do we react to the threatening atmosphere about us? Escape is attractive. Thomas Merton fled from the noise and unhealthiness of his life-style in New York and became a Trappist monk, only to discover that he had taken his own turmoil into the silence of Gethsemane. The story of Jonah makes the point: there is no escaping from oneself, one's God and one's mission.

Another reaction is to do what Christian's young friend Hopeful did, immerse himself with abandon in everything that was going on, enjoying all the 'Treasures and Riches of the World', shutting his eyes to deeper things, until dissatisfaction set in.

Elizabeth Jennings tells us in a poem that she was once one of the many people who try to bar big problems from worrying them. She busied herself with small, mundane matters instead.

> I kept my answers small and I kept them near;
> Big questions bruised my mind but still I let
> Small answers be a bulwark to my fear.
>
> But the big answers clamoured to be moved
> Into my life. Their great audacity
> Shouted to be acknowledged and believed.[3]

A pilgrim is one who seeks answers to big questions about the world and life and self. What starts anyone on the quest remains a mystery. In Christian's case we find him weighed down with the wrongs of his own and the world's life, but, happily for him, holding a key, the Bible, in his hands, for he had overheard a group of women talking together about the Gospel and grace, and decided he wanted to know more.

1. PP p 8.
2. *Op cit* p 121.
3. *Answers* — two verses of the poem.

3. WALKING IN THE FIELDS

Solitude

A change had come over the man, Christian. He would 'walk solitarily in the Fields, sometimes reading, and sometimes praying'. At other times he would retire to 'his Chamber to pray' for his family and himself.[1]

Solitude, reading and reflecting (or meditating) upon the Scriptures, together with prayer, are the foundation of the spiritual way of life and the essence of retreat.

Everyone with but a small acquaintance of the Gospels knows how Jesus, directly after his baptism, went into the desert for forty days to meditate and pray about his ministry, rejecting the overtures of the tempter. And there are other instances of his going apart to a lonely place for prayer. The disciples noted his example and his teaching: 'When you pray, go into a room by yourself, shut the door, and pray to your Father who is there in the secret place.'[2] Nevertheless, busy people should not restrict their spiritual exercises to places of retreat. It proved to be very profitable to the Ethiopian eunuch to be reading and pondering Isaiah when riding in his carriage![3] Christian, then, was following the long and natural tradition of spirituality in retreating to be alone with God.

As we approach the year 2000 the world around us is becoming saturated with noise. Are people afraid of silence? Shopping, driving, studying: all must be accompanied by background music, not always of a restful kind! Cyclists, walkers and gardeners may be seen wired up to their favourite group or symphony orchestra's latest cassette. Or are they afraid of solitude, their own company and thoughts? When not actively engaged, they must be amused by other people, television personalities, journalists, novelists, or by friends and acquaintances, chatting.

When they come to worship, silence is embarrassing. They must be gossiping and joking instead of preparing for God's presence. When the service begins it is often taken with haste, pauses being disliked, the style being influenced more by the entertainment world than we are prepared to recognise.

'Be still, and know that I am God' was the command God gave through the psalmist to the warring, raging peoples.[4] Without solitude and stillness we cannot hear his still small voice. Sir Walter Raleigh begins his poem called *Pilgrim's Way,* with a line every Christian needs to make his own, 'Give me my scallop-shell of quiet'.

At first solitude and silence can be daunting, even dreadful. Confusing thoughts and distractions will 'jump about in my mind like monkeys in a banana tree. Anger and greed begin to show their ugly faces.'[5] In fact we are not alone. The Book in the hand is God's catalyst; our subjective muddle will be gradually straightened out by the Spirit. Just as the sight of human entrails and organs is something of a shock at first, so the exposure of the motivation and primitive feelings of one's inner self is nauseating. Yet to be at peace, to serve God and humanity it has to be faced. It can be faced hand-in-hand with God. As that most profound of the psalms, 139, puts it:

> Search me, O God, and know my heart:
> Try me, and know my thoughts:
> And see if there be any wicked way in me;
> And lead me in the way everlasting.

Distress is unavoidable, but morbidity is not, because the love of God is always lavishing upon us forgiveness and hope.

'Let him who cannot be alone beware of community.' So speaks Dietrich Bonhöffer in his *Life Together.* There are Christians, he says, who cannot stand their own company, who think to find relief for their spirits in Christian fellowship. But their problems cannot be solved unless they will go apart with God, alone, and not simply to perform a ritual act of Bible reading and prayer.

Solitude and silence are essential, not only for the individual, but for the health of society which needs the independence of thought which is its fruit. How is the Spirit to find the opportunity he needs if we all have our ears plugged into something else?

1. PP p 9.
2. Matthew 6:6.
3. Acts 8:28ff.
4. Psalm 46:10
5. Henri Nouwen, *The Way of the Heart*, pp27f.

4. KEEP THAT LIGHT IN YOUR EYE

The Aim

Christian saw how much evil there was in the world about him; he felt the load of sin bearing down upon his own soul; but – what to do about it all?

> I saw . . . that he looked this way and that way, as if he would run; yet he stood still, because, as I perceived, he could not tell which way to go.[1]

Happily, he encountered a sympathetic minister, Evangelist, who heard his cry and gave him direction. This part of the story follows Bunyan's own experience with John Gifford.

Now it has to be frankly admitted that the dialogue between Christian and Evangelist is bound to get a cold reception from the average modern reader. Christian's all-consuming aim is to save his own soul. He is afraid of dying, of judgment and of hell. This fails to strike a chord in most of us. We dislike its egoism and rebel at its crude literalism.

Nevertheless, to be fair to Bunyan, he was only following the current fashion for self-awareness. As Geoffrey Nuttall reminds us, this was the age of Rembrandt, who painted self-portraits, and Descartes, with his 'cogito, ergo sum' philosophy, when people kept diaries and wrote autobiographies. Self-consciousness had been born.[2]

Indeed, are modern people less interested in themselves? Only they do not cry, What shall I do to be saved? but What shall I do to achieve self-fulfilment?

Every child has to learn that to balance on one foot one has to fix one's eye on some stationary object at a distance; the worst thing is to look down at one's wobbling leg. Similarly, inner peace comes when one focuses attention on an object beyond oneself. The question is where to aim.

> Whither must I fly? Then said *Evangelist,* pointing with

> his finger over a very wide Field, Do you see yonder Wicket-gate? The Man said, No. Then said the other, Do you see yonder shining light? He said, I think I do. Then said *Evangelist,* Keep that light in your eye . . .

We should admire Evangelist's sensitivity here. He discerns that the man is not yet ready for commitment (the Wicket-gate) and so he encourages him to follow the light he can see. In Christian's case this shines from the Bible with which he was daily becoming more acquainted: 'Thy word is a lamp unto my feet, and a light unto my path.'[3]

If in the seventeenth century, when Christian ideas were very familiar, there were yet people who found it difficult to grasp the unique significance of Jesus Christ, let alone to commit themselves to his way, then it is far from surprising that in our pagan age the very wide field Christian had to cross to his goal has become more like a strange new territory. What needs to be nurtured is that intermittent spark of hope in the heart, itself a gift of the Spirit, the longing for an absolute good, for a reality outside our world, for light giving purpose and resolution to life.

No words of Jesus apply more to this situation than those recorded in *Matthew 7. 7-8* about seeking and finding. The parables too remind us of the hiddenness of God and his kingdom, for God is wrapt in glory and holiness which no mortal eye can see. The way is only found by searching for it, asking where it is, and finally knocking at the gate when we have arrived. Where those with conviction can help is by comforting and encouraging seekers to keep the light in their eye.

Dag Hammarskjøld's lines reflect the sense of excitement, doubt and hope which he felt as he crossed the 'very wide field'.

> I am being driven forward
> Into an unknown land.
> The pass grows steeper,
> The air colder and sharper.
> A wind from my unknown goal
> Stirs the strings
> Of expectation.

Still the question:
Shall I ever get there?
There where life resounds,
A clear pure note
In the silence.[4]

1 PP p 9.
2 The *Heart of the Pilgrim's Progress* in *Reformation Principle and Practice,* p 231.
3 Psalm 119:103.
4 *Markings,* p 31.

5. HE LOOKED NOT BEHIND HIM

Home Ties

An aspect of *Pilgrim's Progress* which appears to do the author no credit is the way he has Christian uproot himself and desert his family. All the same, we should tease ourselves with the problem facing the author: how to write a story about a man who goes off on a journey whilst remaining all the while at home! The Gospel settled the matter for Bunyan. When Christian's wife and family tried to persuade him not to set out, 'he put his fingers in his Ears, and ran on crying, Life, Life, Eternal Life: so he looked not behind him.'[1] The marginal reference is to *Luke 14.26,* 'If any man come to me, and hate not his father, and mother, and wife and children, and brethren and sisters, yea and his own life also, he cannot be my disciple.'

This saying is one that puzzles many Christians. It is one of several cases where the mere translation of words gives a false impression. Like others of his culture, Jesus liked to speak with astonishing exaggeration to drive home a point. *Matthew 5.29* is another case, where he speaks of plucking out your eye if it offends you. Here, as Kittel assures us, what is meant is the need of 'total commitment that gives priority to Jesus.'[2]

So Bunyan here is saying that the call to pilgrimage has to be obeyed no matter what one's dearest friends and relatives may say. God must be put first. It is most difficult for those Christians whose partners do not share their views and practices; they have to make clear where they stand.

At the time of the Restoration many Dissenters faced painful choices: whether to court imprisonment and maybe transportation. Execution was not likely but death through suffering imprisonment was not uncommon. Bunyan ministered to dying companions. The alternative was to lie low, stay with the family, earn a living, and suffer from a permanently guilty conscience. Bunyan knew without doubt what he had to do, but parting from his wife and family was, he said, 'as the pulling of flesh from the bones'. Most of all, anxiety for his eldest child, blind Mary, broke his heart. To accuse Bunyan then of lack of affection for his own folk is unjust. He attempted to show that Christian loved his family, perhaps not entirely convincingly, by telling the tale of Christiana's pilgrimage.

Christian, in the image of his creator Bunyan, was a modern man who believed in individualism, the rights of the individual. He was not of the old way, the way that expected when the head turned all the rest of the family or tribe or kingdom would turn too. This ancient attitude can be seen in *Acts 16.30ff,* where the gaoler asks Paul and Silas what to do to be saved; they let it creep into their answer: 'Put your trust in the Lord Jesus and you will be saved, you *and your household.'* And, to be sure, he and his household were baptised. Christian was not of this old mind. He pleaded with his wife and family, but he would not harass them; they had to make up their own minds.

Nowadays everyone accepts the individual's rights in such matters — 'he has his own life to live,' we say — yet there are still domineering individuals who exert pressure on others. Their possessive love, so necessary when children are infants, does not fit adult relationships and is utterly unlike God's love which gives us so much freedom. How often Paul's beloved words on love in *1 Corinthians 13.4-7* are read but not grasped, for what do they add up to but acting so that others enjoy their liberty and privacy fully?

In contrast C S Lewis provides us with an exquisite pen portrait of one, Mrs Fidget, who 'lived for her family', and worked 'her fingers to the bone' for them. No one could stop her fussing — till death did. At the funeral the vicar told the family she was now at peace, and they all hoped she was. For the first time they knew they were![3] Some advice von Hügel wrote his niece is worth pondering. 'The golden rule is to help those we love escape from us, and never try to begin to help people, or influence them till they ask.'.

The difficulties of Christians living in secular families ought not to be exaggerated whilst the tensions there can be in a Christian family, where some are rather too wrapt up in the world's cares and pleasures, are brushed under the carpet. In any case, a large part of every Christian's pilgrimage has to be alone.

1. PP pp 9f.
2. G W Bromiley, *Theological Dictionary of the New Testament,* p 598f.
3. *Four Loves,* 'Man is not a Hothouse Plant.'

6. SLOUGH OF DESPOND

Disappointment

Accompanied by a friend called Pliable, Christian made a good start on his pilgrimage. Obstinate was left behind; he could only be derisive and rude. Time was passed very pleasantly, Christian enjoying telling Pliable about the glories of the coming Kingdom in great detail, using a multitude of biblical texts. Pliable felt encouraged by this to press on faster but Christian protested that his burden made this impossible. Talking subsided and

> they drew near to a very *Miry Slow* that was in the midst of the Plain, and they being heedless, did both fall suddenly into the bogg. The name of the Slow was *Dispond.* Here therefore they wallowed for a time, being grievously bedaubed with dirt; And *Christian,* because of the burden that was on his back, began to sink in the *Mire.*
>
> *Pli. Then said* Pliable, Ah, Neighbour Christian, *where are you now?*
>
> *Chr.* Truly, said *Christian,* I do not know.
>
> *Pli.* At that *Pliable* began to be offended; and angerly, said to his Fellow, *Is this the happiness you have told me all this while of?*[1]

Disgusted, Pliable struggled out of the bog and 'away he went, and Christian saw him no more'. Christian struggled on. Unhappily he missed the stepping stones which Christiana used (forgiveness and renewal).

It is not uncommon for beginners in the spiritual life, once the excitement of launching out has worn off, to experience a reaction. It is a sad disappointment to find that sinfulness persists; it has not been left behind. In *Grace Abounding to the Chief of Sinners,* Bunyan records that his time of contrition was long and painful. 'I found myself in a miry bog,' he says, 'left of God.' His prayer for Christ to call him out of it seemed unheard. Good friends assured him that God's promises to forgive and renew penitents were meant for him but he remained deaf. 'They had as good have told me that I must reach the sun with my finger.' He saw no stepping-stones. All he knew was that he had 'a heart that would sin'.[2]

Such painful honesty is rare. As the actor Sir Ralph Richardson used to say, 'A person is a whole pack of cards.'[3] Power and work, wealth and sex motivate us; we are full of good intentions and bad tricks; we play our parts with kings, queens and knaves, as well as mediocre and weak efforts. Self-examination is necessary and healthy if it is conducted prayerfully in the presence of Christ, the Great Physician. But without him it can lead down into dark caverns full of terror. This was Bunyan's state for too long, so that in the end, utterly exhausted, he wanted to curse Christ and die.

Disappointment and dejection cloud our lives from time to time. Many a theological student who has begun training full of enthusiasm has tasted disillusion within a year. Ministers in new pastorates have seen their hopes dashed. Dean Matthews tells us how he proposed in 1946 that St Paul's Cathedral should have a band of Friends to help with the rebuilding. Exeter and Canterbury already did. But for six years the clergy poured cold water on the idea, fearing a lay take-over, and when at last it was formed, it was really too late on the scene.[4] Life is a graveyard full of dashed hopes.

The danger is of disappointment settling into despondency and eventually bitterness. This is a sign of spiritual immaturity, a refusal to accept the cross. To be broken-hearted in such circumstances can be the opportunity to learn humility, to become Christ-centred, and thus more tenacious than before. However, we must add that sometimes dejection is simply the consequence of over-work or the onset of a virus.

Happily for Christian someone called Help arrived. *'Then, said he, Give me thy hand;* so he gave him his hand, and he drew him out, and set him upon sound ground and bid him go his way.'

> Christ leads me through no darker rooms
> Than he went through before.[5]

1. PP pp 12ff
2. *Op cit,* paras 73-82.
3. Garry O'Connor, *Ralph Richardson,* p 207.
4. *Memories and Meanings,* pp 33f.
5. Richard Baxter, *Congregational Praise,* no 435.

7. MR WORLDLY-WISEMAN

Religion

'How now, good fellow, whither away after this burdened manner?' Thus Mr Worldly-Wiseman greets Christian and soon he is offering him the friendliest advice on how to be rid of his distressing burden.[1] This man is not worldly in the sense of being materialistic or indulging the appetites, let alone displaying coarseness. Indeed, he is urbane, thoroughly at home in polite society and every inch respectable. You may meet his like in many a church.

He closely questions Christian, barely taking in his replies. Has he a wife and children? Well, he shouldn't have left them. Who set him on the Christian way? He shouldn't have taken any notice of the 'dangerous and troublesome' counsel of Evangelist, a perfect stranger to him. And what gave him the idea of pilgrimage anyway? The Book! For ordinary people it is 'meddling with things too high' to study the Bible.

However, he can be rid of his burden. He can be happy and honoured, and carry his family along with him. The solution is to keep the moral law and live a decent life.

Christian is persuaded. He makes off in the direction of the village of Morality but becomes apprehensive where the road is overhung by a high hill. This represents the Old Testament Law. And then there appears on the road Evangelist, bearing 'a severe and dreadful countenance', barring the way, wanting to know why he has gone astray.

Evangelist takes Christian in hand, admonishes him, counsels him and sets him back in the right direction, towards the Wicket-gate.

The narrative suggests that the whole episode occupies but an afternoon. In Bunyan's life it took a year. In *Grace Abounding* he speaks of his 'outward reformation' and how amazed neighbours were at his 'great conversion'. He himself became pleased 'mighty well' with his godliness. 'I thought I pleased God as well as any man in England,' he says, 'though I knew not Christ, nor grace, nor faith, nor hope'. Now and again he erred, promised to do better, failed again. At last he suspected that he was 'nothing but a poor painted hypocrite'.[2]

The Worldly-Wiseman type is more often found outside the Church today. This person asserts that you don't have to go to church to be a Christian. Religion consists of doing your best, maybe saying a prayer, and keeping your nose clean.

Within the Church, among keen Christians, a near relative of Worldly-Wiseman is often found. This is the person devoted to a formula or practice for daily living which is believed to be the way of salvation, providing one sticks to it faithfully. It may be a Daily Office or regimen of Bible reading and prayer. It may turn into a barren routine but the discipline of keeping it is what matters, what pleases God. And so the weed Pharisaism spreads. After most of a lifetime as a Trappist monk, Thomas Merton says experience taught him that it is impossible to set up 'a kind of laboratory for prayer' which will produce the grace desired to order.[3]

This is not to dismiss either the rules of morality or methods of devotion as unimportant. Paul teaches us to see in the Law a tutor and all the saints testify to the need of disciplined Bible reading, meditation and lively prayer. But they are tools for salvation, not ends in themselves. The way through the little Wicket-gate is the way to freedom and there we must go.

1. PP pp 16ff.
2. *Op cit*, paras 30-32.
3. *Contemplation in a World of Action*, p 102.

8. THE WICKET-GATE

Conversion

'In the process of time Christian got up to the Gate.' In fact it was a solid door. Over it was a notice which recited *Matthew 7.8,* 'Knock and it shall be opened unto you.' So he knocked and 'at last there came a grave Person' who asked him his business, and after Christian had related that he was 'a poor burdened sinner' travelling from the City of Destruction to Mount Zion and asked if he was willing to admit him, the gate-keeper exclaimed, 'I am *willing* with all my heart' and pulled him in. There were enemies lurking in the vicinity who longed to shoot pilgrims down.[1]

The Wicket-gate is derived from *Matthew 7.13-14,* 'Enter ye in at the strait gate . . . which leadeth unto life.' This text, says Keeble, the Puritans took to mean 'the experience of conversion and regeneration, the only possible beginning to an authentic Christian life'.[2] It is only fair, however, to add that spiritual leaders from all over the Church, people as different as St Ignatius de Loyola and Martin Luther, have held much the same view.

Some time later, Christian met one, Ignorance, who considered himself a disciple and listed his credentials, and he challenged him thus: 'But thou camest not in at the Wicket-Gate.'[3] Good behaviour, prayers and generosity (works) are inadequate as a preparation for Eternal Life which requires faith. This faith comes by way of effort: searching within and without, and questioning too, knocking at many doors until the right one is opened.

That Bunyan is not precise regarding the details of conversion is a sign of his wisdom, people being so varied. Christiana with her 'sweet babes' almost sweeps through and a trumpet sounds, but Mercie, trailing a little behind, finds the door shut in her face. The trouble is that she is not quite sure why she came on the pilgrimage, save to keep beside her good friend. The shock of being outside and alone stirs her profoundly and she knocks desperately for entry, but when it is opened, is found swooning on the ground and has to be revived and led in.[4] On the other hand,

Mr Fearing, who suffers from a *'Slow of Dispond* in his Mind' dithers endlessly and is eventually fetched in![5]

Dawdling on the brink of decision is understandably common. Many, like Augustine of Hippo, say, 'Not yet,' for they cannot break with 'the baggage of this present world.'[6] Others, like C S Lewis, find it a hard struggle to give up their independence of will to God, whom he called 'the transcendental interferer'.[7]

Nor is Bunyan specific in identifying the gate-keeper. He seems to want to hide his identity. Only in Mr Fearing's case is it undoubtedly Christ. In Christian's the man is called Good-Will. It is later on that he learns how to discern Christ. One is reminded of the great change that came about in Dag Hammarskjøld's life when he said 'Yes to Someone', and existence took on a meaning and his life 'in self-surrender, had a goal'.[8] Can people be expected always to define the power keeping the door?

The name Good-Will is of utmost importance. Conversion according to the Bible means turning. Christian turned from fear and misery to find in God good-will. He found a warm welcome, a call away from his old collapsed style of life to new life. Of course, he still had a long way to go before he would be totally changed.

1. PP pp 2ff.
2. PP p 265.
3. PP p 101.
4. PP pp 155f.
5. PP pp 207f.
6. *Confessions,* VIII, 11.
7. *Surprised by Joy,* p 163.
8. *Markings,* p 169.

9. THE INTERPRETER'S HOUSE: BY THE HAND

Feelings

Christian's next destination was the Interpreter's House.[1] After knocking more than once, someone answered the door and asked him his business. He explained the nature of his journey and said he'd been told that if he called there he'd be shown 'excellent things, such as would be an help' on the journey. 'Come in,' replied the Interpreter. What follows may well owe much to Bunyan's recollections of his own initial Christian instruction under John Gifford at St John the Baptist Rectory, Bedford. Gifford was a man of wide experience and sympathies. Before becoming pastor to the Independent congregation he had been a major in the Royalist army, had been captured, condemned to death, had escaped from prison, gone underground and later emerged as a physician in Bedford!

As the two went from room to room we must observe 'he took him by the hand and led him'. The importance of the action is shown by its repetition six times. It conveys to us the atmosphere in which instruction takes place: the friendliness and gentleness of Interpreter.

Throughout *Pilgrim's Progress* there is a refreshing naturalness about people. They are not afraid to show one another their feelings. Indeed sentiments are not so much expressed in speech as in gestures.

Tears are nothing to be ashamed of. When his burden fell from his back as he gazed upon the cross, where he imagined he saw Jesus hanging, 'the springs that were in his head sent the waters down his cheeks'.[2] When he came to the Palace Beautiful, the Church, and wanted to join, there is no actual mention of his formal acceptance. What we read, however, is that Prudence, on hearing his request, smiled and 'the water stood in her eyes'.[3] A stoical bearing, never showing emotion, did not appeal to Bunyan or his age. What a pity it is that more sermons haven't sentiments like Philip Doddridge's *Meditation on the Tears of Jesus* where he says,

> Surely when God implanted in our Nature these

melting Emotions of the Soul, he intended them for some valuable Purpose, and not that we should look upon them as Weeds, to be rooted out of every well cultivated Soil.

Look at old Honest, a Dickensian character, who was so thrilled to meet Christiana — he had known her from of old — that 'he skip't, he smiled, and blessed them with a thousand good Wishes'. And he kissed them all with the holy kiss of charity.[4] Notice also that Evangelist, after he had sternly reproved Christian for going astray towards the village of Morality, as he set him in the right direction, 'kist him, gave him one smile, and bid him God speed'.[5]

And why not express our feelings to God our Father?

George Downame was someone whose writing had a great influence on Bunyan. Whether Bunyan followed his directions on physical postures for prayer or not one cannot say, but he recommended standing for praise, kneeling or prostration for the confession of sins, sitting for meditation; also raising and lowering the eyes to indicate aspiration and dejection, provided care be taken to 'give God in truth inward worship of the soul as well as outward of the body'.[6] Isaac Watts believed in very similar postures for prayer.[7] It all helps feeling.

Bunyan also teaches people to do more than listen to others, to watch and read the signs. Poor Mr Fearing is inarticulate. He is lost for words when he arrives at the Interpreter's House, but Great-heart notices the tears in his eyes and arranges his admission. Another, different, example is that of Madame Bubble. Stand-fast and Honest watch how she keeps fingering money in her purse and how she rounds off her smooth speech with a smile, and they are rightly suspicious. Esther de Waal does well to remind modern people to listen with 'body as well as the intellect' and 'with love as well as cerebral assent'.[8]

1. PP pp 23ff.
2. PP p 31.
3. PP p 39.
4. PP p 206.
5. PP p 20.
6. *A Godly and Learned Treatise of Prayer*, pp 120ff.
7. *Guide to Prayer*.
8. *Seeking God*, p 42.

10. THE PICTURE

Our Christ

What basic teaching does a new Christian need? Bunyan's answer is unfolded in the Interpreter's House.

As our Lord taught in parables, Bunyan taught with word pictures. Indeed, when teaching children he used wood-cuts as a visual aid. Books illustrated with them were popular in those days; we call them Emblem Books.

The house was dark and it was necessary to light a candle to find the way safely. Do we not commence instruction nowadays with a prayer for illumination by the Holy Spirit?

The first exhibit pilgrims are shown is a large portrait hanging on a wall. It shows 'a very grave Person'.[1] 'Grave' meant important, notable, in those times; not serious, bearing bad or troublesome news. The figure

> had eyes lift up to Heaven, the best of Books in its hand, the Law of Truth was written upon its lips, the World was behind its back; it stood as if it pleaded with Men, and a Crown of Gold did hang over its head.

Who is this? We want to know and so did Christian, but no clear answer is given. Bunyan, like our Lord, had a habit of not giving direct answers but giving a few clues and leaving the hearer to make up his own mind. The Interpreter goes on to say that this man 'can beget children', and moreover, 'nurse them himself when they are born'. He unfolds 'dark things to sinners'. 'I have showed thee this Picture first,' he says, 'because the Man whose Picture this is, is the only Man, whom the Lord of the Place whither thou art going, hath Authorised, to be thy Guide . . .' Commentators have interpreted this picture to be that of the minister, and yet it is very hard to believe that the Interpreter was talking about himself or even the ministry in general in such high and mighty terms. All the biblical references are to the Apostle Paul. Does it represent him? It remains something of a mystery but it also bears a striking resemblance to Christ himself, the only way to the Father.

In any case it is a picture. At the Reformation religious art took a severe beating. Didn't the second commandment ban images? Didn't our Lord say God is spirit and we must worship him in spirit and in truth? Any visual representation of God, Father, Son or Holy Spirit, seemed therefore to be flouting the Word of God and inviting superstition.

The problem is that people see the Christ that they want to see. As William Blake put it, with some wit:

> The Vision of Christ that thou dost see
> Is my Vision's Greatest Enemy:
> Thine has a great hook nose like thine,
> Mine has a snub nose like to mine.[3]

As the Roman world turned towards Christianity, we find the Good Shepherd depicted as a young Apollo. In the Middle Ages we have El Greco painting Christ as an ascetic – he wasn't. Michelangelo was spell-bound by the human physique of Christ. The opposite is true of Graham Sutherland who in his Coventry Cathedral tapestry seems to be reviving the otherworldly, ikon style of the Orthodox Church. The way the stage and screen portray Christ in our day is always bound to stir up debate.

Nonconformist churches have never faced the issue squarely. It is a weird logic that welcomes pictures of Christ in schoolrooms, Bibles and studies, but not in places of worship.

One thing is certain, however. We have to do our best to make new Christians knowledgeable about Jesus Christ, disabusing them of false pictures, and above all trying to impress upon them the centrality of Christ, the only way to God the Father. Each must make his own ikon.

1. PP p 24.
2. John 4:24.
3. *Everlasting Gospel.*

11. EMBLEMS

Principles

Once the pilgrims have a thorough grounding in the first principle, the Lordship of Christ, which necessarily involves the consideration of the nature of God, they move on to the second principle: the salvation of man.

The Interpreter takes Christian to witness an amusing scene. A clumsy man goes into a room to sweep it clean but manages to raise a cloud of dust so thick that it begins to choke Christian. It requires a woman with common sense to come in and damp down the dust before sweeping. 'What means this?' asks Christian. The dust symbolises sin; the sweeper is Law, which only manages to stir it up; then comes the woman, 'the sweet Grace of the Gospel,' who overcomes sin.[1] Such an old-fashioned model will not do in the age of vacuum cleaners, but whatever story we invent, we must grapple with the same issues, with the meaning and purpose of life and how anyone can become a whole person.

Today, as Mary Stocks says, you may say that someone has been foolish or misguided but not wicked, and to mention sin would appear 'priggish or hypocritical or Victorian'. To think that individuals need sometimes to 'experience a sense of guilt' for the sake of social morality is against the tide.[2] The difficulty is compounded by the superficial notion of sin which most folk have. John Baillie takes us to the root of the matter, to pride itself.

> Each of us behaves as if all things were centred in humanity and humanity in him. I *will* not see that I am no more important than the man next door. England *will* not see that she is no more important than her continental neighbours . . . Man *will* not see that his importance lies not in himself but in his relationship to God.[3]

In fact human beings are a tangle of good and evil. Think of biblical heroes like David and Peter. Or walk round an old cathedral and observe how symbols of good and evil jostle each other: crosses and swords, the lamb with his flag and the proud arms of conquerors. The wonder is that good has never been annihilated. And so Christian is shown a man pouring water on a fire. Yet the fire burns up more than before. It is against a wall and when Christian is taken behind it he sees someone busy feeding the fire with oil through a hole in the wall! It's another version of Jesus' parable of the wheat and tares (weeds).[4] The survival of good in life is due to the activity of the Holy Spirit.

We haven't room to touch upon all the emblems. One will be the subject of the next section, but two need mentioning here because they concern an aspect of traditional doctine which Christians of all persuasions used to stress and now neglect, namely damnation. One scene showed a frightened man who had a nightmare about the Last Judgment. He was not frightened of the demons; but by his own stained conscience. The other was the doomed man in an iron cage who had committed the unforgivable sin. Once a good Christian, he had so indulged in 'the Lusts, Pleasures, and Profits of this World' that he had reached the point of no return. Christian was dismayed. Surely no one is beyond salvation? But the man said God had denied him repentance. He could no more be restored than a gangrened limb.

It is most doubtful if the fear of hell ever made good Christians. Jesus himself took damnation for granted but chose positive features of the Kingdom to appeal to hearers. Nevertheless, are we not guilty of passing over an important question if we fail to consider whether judgment isn't necessary, whether holiness doesn't require a hygienic barrier around the Kingdom of Heaven? What else does *Hebrews* mean by saying that our God is a consuming fire?[5]

1. PP pp 24f.
2. *Still More Commonplace,* p 108.
3. *Invitation to Pilgrimage,* Chap 8.
4. Matthew 13:25ff.
5. Hebrews 12:29.

12. WHO WOULD TRUE VALOUR SEE

Fighting Spirit

'I think I know the meaning of this,' remarked Christian when the Interpreter showed him an armed man 'of a very stout countenance' who cut his way through massed opposition and entered the King's Palace.[1]

Puritans made good soldiers and colonists, 'prepared for the worst', says Perry Miller; there was nothing 'lukewarm, half-hearted or flabby' about them.[2] Here is an aspect of our ancestry to be proud of.

The imagery of soldiering and warfare has always been popular among Christians for describing the spiritual and moral struggle. Hymns with bright marching tunes are sung every Sunday, though some people mumble them unconvincingly, oppressed by the twentieth century's unparalleled record of violence.

Jürgen Moltmann has suggested that the artist might be substituted for the soldier.[3] The artist too must be highly trained and single-minded, indeed 'of a very stout countenance'. Recall Picasso in his early days, exploring his new style of painting — painting as a form of writing — when friends deserted him, convinced he would go mad and kill himself. But he stuck at it and won through.[4]

However, that the artist could ever take the soldier's place in Christian imagery is not credible. The fact is that we have not all got artistic talents, whereas we all have and we all need fighting instincts, or we should not survive illness, pass examinations or win games, let alone oppose evil. The Church did not earn the epithet 'Militant' for nothing. Fighting injustice and callousness was born into it from its prophetic forebears and this has been carried forward ever since as is witnessed by the medieval orders of chivalry and the list of social reformers in more recent times.

Whether our churches are prepared for exhausting and painful warfare against evil today is open to question. It was early in the last century that Kierkegaard complained that his Church was only 'playing at Christianity' and 'pretending that it is Christianity that is taught.' The worship, the preaching and the fellowship he summed up as 'a diluted and effeminate sentimentality.'[5] Thomas Merton in this century has the same complaint. He accuses the Church of being 'too intimately connected with ideas of "peace" and psychological conduct'.[6] Those among us responsible for ministerial settlements say that congregations usually seek pastoral comfort rather than spiritual leadership from their ministers.

We also generally assume that the practice of private prayer should be peaceful, relaxing and contemplative. Does it mean that we are retreating from reality? Here we find the lonely voice of P T Forsyth warning us that we should be expecting tension, anguish and strife in our prayer life because of the times we live in. With alarm he exposes those who teach congregations 'pietist fatalism' which 'thins the spiritual life' and 'saps the vigour of character', and makes 'humility mere acquiescence'. There are times when prayer must be wrestling, as Jacob found. Forsyth does not hesitate to assert that 'prayer may change the will of God'. God is 'an infinite opportunist', who likes changing things for those who wrestle in prayer. Probably few Christians feel as confident about this as Forsyth, yet there are many who are sure that an essential part of prayer is struggling to discern the right way, the will of God. Forsyth urges us to take to heart Meredith's criticism:

> The curse of so much religion is that men cling to God with their weakness rather than their strength.[7]

No one can read *Pilgrim's Progress* without realising that the Christian life, ardently lived, is for tough people.

1. PP p 27.
2. *The Puritans*, p 60.
3. *An Invitation to an Open Messianic Life Style*, chap 3.
4. Daniel-Henry Kahnweiler, *My Galleries and Painters*.
5. *Last Years*, p 30.
6. *The Plaster Saint*, pp 97f.
7. *The Soul of Prayer*, chap 7.

13. THE BURDEN AND THE CROSS

Symbolism

Two very different pictures of Christian appear in *Pilgrim's Progress*: a fleeing refugee, in rags, half running, half staggering under a great burden; the other, well-robed and armed, unburdened, hasting steadily forwards. The astonishing transformation takes place soon after he has left the Interpreter's House where he has received his basic instruction as a Christian.

> Now I saw in my dream that the high way up which Christian was to go, was fenced on either side with a Wall, and that Wall is called *Salvation.* Up this way therefore did burdened *Christian* run, but not without great difficulty, because of the load on his back.
>
> He ran thus till he came at a place somewhat ascending; and upon that place stood a Cross, and a little below in the bottom, a Sepulcher. So I saw in my Dream, that just as *Christian* came up with the Cross, his burden loosed from off his Shoulders, and fell from off his back; and began to tumble; and so continued to do, till it came to the mouth of the Sepulcher, where it fell in, and I saw it no more.
>
> Then was *Christian* glad and lightsom, and said with a merry heart, *He hath given me rest, by his sorrows; and life by his death.*[1]

Shining ones saluted him, pronounced his sins forgiven, dressed him in new clothes, marked his forehead and presented him with a Roll with a seal on it.

But why did he have to wait so long before losing his burden of guilt? At the Wicket-gate he had begged Good-Will to help him off with it, only to be told to have patience: 'Be content to bear it, until thou comest to the place of Deliverance.'[2]

The fact is that it takes time for the Gospel to sink in and for terms like grace and forgiveness to lose their cool abstraction and become personal, meaningful, alive. How long this melancholy phase took Bunyan is related in his autobiographical *Grace Abounding to the Chief of Sinners.*

In the eyes of an average person his sins were not all that serious, certainly not criminal, but they threw him into a state of desperation. William James called him psychotic.[3] Bunyan at the time, like many of us, was mistaking self-pity for penitence. What is needed is to heed Staupitz's warning to Martin Luther, 'Do not brood over your sins.'[4] The puritan preacher Richard Sibbes puts it picturesquely saying 'we may fix our eyes too long upon sin itself' and thus 'weave the web of our own sorrow'.[5]

Many of us find forgiveness a brook hard to leap across. Dag Hammarskjøld points out that it's difficult, maybe impossible to forgive oneself; that is where the problem often begins. 'To forgive oneself —? No, that doesn't work.' And therefore 'we have to *be forgiven.*' But is this possible? Hammarskjøld shows a way: 'we can only believe this is possible if we ourselves can forgive.'[6]

Surely the world would grind to a halt without forgiveness. In his prayer our Lord is saying that just as we need our rations day by day, so we need forgiveness to make the daily round and common task blessed. Forgiveness begins with a multitude of minor acts of forbearance, seventy times seven and over, through to momentous sacrifices.

Whilst we all need forgiveness, not many of us have to travel the lonely, stormy route to it Bunyan experienced. He was wise enough to know this and therefore he had Christiana, when she saw the cross, react quite differently from her husband. She did not exult in a sense of freedom She was filled with wonder.

> Methinks it makes my heart bleed to think that he should bleed for me. Oh! thou loving one, Oh! thou blessed one.[7]

Moreover, it may be a comfort to some that Faithful in his account of his spiritual adventures makes mention of neither burden nor cross! Bunyan is no narrow evangelical.

Indeed, it could be argued that Bunyan is a bad Puritan. Underneath he belongs to the great Church catholic. Puritans, especially Dissenters, had no time for symbols. How is it then that seeing a cross effects in a moment what hours of discourse could not do? Of course, empty symbolism fosters superstition, but meaningful symbolism says what words cannot say.

1. PP p 31.
2. PP p 23.
3. *Varieties of Religious Experience*, (1945 ed) p 154.
4. John M Todd, *Luther: A Life*, p 217.
5. *The Soul's Conflict*, published sermon.
6. *Markings*, p 133.
7. PP p 175.

14. THE HILL DIFFICULTY

Choices

C S Lewis once remarked, 'If you want a religion to make you feel really comfortable, I certainly don't recommend Christianity.'[1] Christian had no illusions on this score and was not in the least surprised to see 'a steep and high hill' before him. To be sure, there was an easy path going round to the left and another to the right, but 'the narrow way lay right up the Hill', which was aptly named Difficulty.[2]

Surely it is no accident that Bunyan locates this hill close upon the pilgrim's joyful experiences at the cross and in the Interpreter's house. By now the pilgrim had learnt enough about Christ and himself to have a sharpened conscience and a mind able to discern between choices.

Then two other pilgrims joined Christian and the three conferred about the way to go. These two chose the easy ways, for they were wedded to comfortable religion. One got lost in a wood and the other among dark mountains, 'where he stumbled and fell, and rose no more.' In any event, neither Formalist nor Hypocrisy had entered by the Wicket-gate but taken instead a popular short-cut over a wall.[3] Christian went straight ahead.

The pilgrims' three choices remind one of St Ignatius de Loyola's teaching where he says his thoughts were of three sorts, 'one my own, arising from my own free choice, the other two coming from outside, one from the good spirit, the other from the bad spirit.'[4] Who cannot recognise this process in one's mind? Perhaps modern readers may hesitate to say whether certain ideas come from outside. We should, nonetheless, be able to discern which thoughts are derived from Christian teaching and which reflect the 'old Adam'.

Had Bunyan any particular event in his life in mind when he wrote about this hill? Was he recalling the day he was arrested in November 1660? At the Restoration an Elizabethan law forbidding conventicles, ie religious meetings outside the parish church, had been re-imposed.

Bunyan was warned that the farm where he was to preach was being watched and that a warrant for his arrest had been issued, and friends begged him to postpone his visit, but he remained resolute. 'No, by no means,' he replied, 'I will not stir, neither will I have the meeting dismissed for this.' In consequence he suffered arrest and spent most of the next twelve years in gaol.

Let us also note what Christiana said of those who choose the easy way: 'They are Idle, they love not to take Pains, up-hill-way is unpleasant to them.'[5]

We are mistaken to apply Bunyan's message too narrowly, just to the obvious moral and spiritual choices of life, to restrict it to a part and not the whole of our activity. Michael Ayrton, one of the best writers on art, contrasts the precise draughtsmanship of Degas with that of Cézanne, who was, he judges, 'shakey', and Bonnard, who was 'hesitant', and attributes it to Degas' struggle to master the drawing of movement. He goes on to warn students not to draw what they find pleasing, but to tackle problems.[6]

Richard Baxter sees it as our Christian duty to 'choose the greatest work, though it be accompanied with the greatest difficulties and suffering'.[7] We overhear our pilgrim as he climbs the hill versifying:

> This Hill, though high, I covet to ascend,
> The difficulty will not me offend:
> For I perceive the way to life lies here;
> Come, pluck up, Heart, lets neither faint nor fear:
> Better, tho difficult, th' right way to go,
> Than wrong, though easie, where the end is wo.

1. *Undeceptions,* p 34.
2. PP pp 34f.
3. PP p 32.
4. *The Spiritual Exercises,* no 32.
5. PP p 178.
6. *Golden Selections,* p 65.
7. *The Reformed Pastor,* p 66.

15. THE ARBOUR

Our Flesh

Christian was a novice at climbing steep hills. He began the ascent too fast, running; he ended up scrambling on all fours. He reached the arbour half way up the hill but set no time-limit on his rest — he wouldn't have had a watch in any case. He thought he would have a read for a little while and took out his Roll, and, of course, 'fell into a slumber, and thence into a fast sleep . . . and in his sleep his Roll fell out of his hand.'[1] He thought someone woke him up and was astonished to find it was evening. So he hurried off uphill, leaving his Roll under the bench. Later on, when he felt for it, it was gone. He had lost his passport to the Kingdom.

Greatly vexed, he retraced his steps, examining the ground as he went, all the while muttering to himself, '*O wretched Man that I am,* that I should sleep in the day time! that I should sleep in the midst of difficulty! that I should so indulge the flesh!' Happily, his Roll was still lying where it fell at the arbour and he retrieved it joyfully.

Everyone must have had similar mishaps and felt equally cross and anxious. What makes Christian different is his Protestant horror at his idleness. By the way, the one who woke him up admonished him with a text from *Proverbs,* a favourite with school teachers up to the close of the last century: 'Go to the Ant, thou sluggard, consider her ways, and be wise.'[2] The Evangelical Revival reinforced this attitude. As William Wilberforce said: 'be active, useful, generous towards others . . . be ashamed of idleness as . . . of the most acknowledged sin.'[3]

Whilst sloth is indefensible and work is much to be valued, Protestants seem to have pressed the point too hard. Baxter was too wise to uphold an extreme view. He counselled Christians not to deny their bodies 'all delight' for 'if the body have none, the mind will have less'. 'A holy improvement of lawful pleasure is a daily duty.'[4]

It is only comparatively recently that the pace and style of life have compelled us to change our attitude to leisure.

Physical activity was the common lot from the dawn of civilisation. Even professional people like doctors and pastors used to spend much of their time riding or walking about their duties. But today work is massively sedentary and travel too, whilst overworking endangers health and happiness. Exercise and leisure must be cultivated.

Charles Darwin, living at the time when the machine was making its take-over bid, found his mind turned into 'a kind of machine for grinding out general laws out of large collections of facts,' and he regretted it. Had he been able to have his time over again, he said, he would want more time for relaxation, for poetry and music.[5]

Balance is what we need. One of the virtues of the Rule of St Benedict is the way he planned the day for his communities, with time for prayer, study and physical work. Esther de Waal, who has done so much to revive interest in the Rule, says, 'we need to remind ourselves . . . that we are essentially rhythmic creatures and that life needs this rhythm and balance.'[6]

1. PP pp 35f.
2. Proverbs 6:6.
3. *A Practical View*, p 486.
5. Christian Directory, II p 217 (ed Orme).
5. *Autobiography*, p 132.
6. *Seeking God*, p 93.

16. THE PALACE BEAUTIFUL

The Church

'No lion can him fright,' we sing in John Bunyan's most famous hymn. What did these lions represent? They stood on the highway to the Palace Beautiful and they represented the fears which pilgrims had to overcome in order to join the Church. In Bunyan's England, as in far too many places abroad today, persecution had to be faced. When Christian hesitated the porter at the Palace cried loudly, 'Is thy strength so small? Fear not the Lions, for they are chained.'[1]

Of course, there are other fears which deter people from joining the Church. Commonly it is fear of one's peers, even one's own family. Another familiar objection is the fear that one will not be able to live up to Christian standards. What a lamentable understanding of the grace of Christ this shows! Perhaps the truth is that the person is afraid of the humiliation to be faced when companions expose the selfishness and weakness which persist despite the claim to be a disciple. How pride is going to be hurt! But remember that the lions are chained. Neither persecution nor humiliation can separate us from the love of Christ, but fear can.

'Trembling for fear of the Lions,' Christian picked his way between them safely and, clapping his hands, reached the Palace and sought lodging. The porter summoned a grave and beautiful damsel, named Discretion, who questioned him closely – a reference to the screening of candidates for church membership among Dissenters — and when she was satisfied, she broke into a smile and fetched her companions, Prudence, Piety and Charity, who, after more discussion, invited him to meet the family. Christian 'bowed his head.' It is remarkable that Bunyan, a roving tinker with little education, is always particular about good manners.

It's a welcoming church. Guests are received with something to drink; a meal is soon on the table; there is a bed for the night in a room named Peace. When Christiana and her party come along, we note that each is welcomed with a kiss by the 'friends.'

In this allegory Bunyan is giving us his own impression of church fellowship at its best. He does not lecture us, teaching us doctrine. He does not mention worship, sacraments or church government. He knows that doctrine has its place but that in the end it is the quality of church fellowship that counts most to the average newcomer.

It must be admitted that a good deal of what Bunyan wrote concerning the Palace Beautiful is tedious and sometimes bizarre. There is a comical account of Mathew's sickness which is cured by the wonderful Dr Skill and his amazing pills and the tale of Mercie's love-affair with Mr Brisk, a carnal fellow who disapproves of Mercie's charitable work and tries to wean her off it; everyone is troubled when they learn of it. And yet this kind of talk is typical of what one hears in the church kitchen over the washing-up!

Questions which members put to Christian are by no means dead. They want to know where his wife is and why she isn't with him. They want to know how he overcomes temptation and masters anxiety; and what does he think of life after death. Serious questions which also figure on the agenda at washing-up sessions.

The prevailing atmosphere, however, is that of joy and friendliness.

Christiana's party, like a good church, contains all sorts and conditions of men. In *One Man's Testimony* Norman Goodall points out and pays tribute to the way an ordinary church enables people of differing tastes, sympathies and views to live together as friends. They are held together by Christ despite serious tension and strain at times.

This he found to be true not only in the Methodist church of his childhood and youth but equally in the international field where he spent so much of his working life. The 'open door to Christian fellowship,' he concludes, 'is available to all and sundry — the door of a very average local church.'[2]

1. PP pp 38ff and 181ff.
2. *Op cit*, pp 73ff.

17. THE ARMOURY

Spiritual Life

Christian was shown the Palace Armoury with its vast collection of swords, shields, breastplates, indeed every armament a pilgrim could want. 'All-Prayer' gets a special mention although Bunyan cannot manage to attach any physical description to it.[1] For all this his source is, of course, *Ephesians 6:14-18,* which introduces us to the fundamentals of the spiritual life.

(1) Inner truth — the belt, omitted by Bunyan, probably because the Authorised Version of the Bible is imprecise. The spiritual life begins with the person being open to the searching Spirit of God which exposes self-deception and all pretences.

(2) Righteousness — the breastplate or coat of mail. Thoughts, words and deeds are to be inspired by uprightness and justice.

(3) The Gospel of Peace — shoes. In the words of *The Jerusalem Bible,* 'eagerness to spread the gospel of peace' which directs where one is to go and what one is to do. It means peace-making, peace-keeping and planting oases of peace in dry places as well as being a well of peace oneself.

(4) Faith — the shield. Roman soldiers were protected by great shields made of wood covered with hide. Faith acts like a shield when arrows of disappointment, sorrow, suffering, doubt and fear assail the Christian.

(5) Salvation — the helmet. Helmets and hats have always been decorated with colours and badges to identify the wearers. The world should see clearly that the Christian stands for God who is a Saviour. *Colossians 3:17* says, 'Whatever you are doing, whether you speak or act, do everything in the name of the Lord Jesus.' We are on the Lord's side, not our own.

(6) God's word — the sword of the Spirit. This is the only weapon of the spiritual fighter. If this is too narrowly inter-

preted, as it has been sometimes, it leads to shying texts at people, which seldom produces the desired effect. Christians have to be more skilful at getting God's message across. How wonderful Jesus was at this, using parables.[2]

It is a pity Bunyan failed to tell us more about 'All-Prayer.' Instead he sent Christian wandering around the Armoury examining museum pieces such as the sling and stone David used to slay Goliath. All this does is illustrate how quickly the spiritual nature of Christian warfare is forgotten and physical triumphs take over.

It is one of the perplexing facts about *Pilgrim's Progress* that prayer is only touched upon now and again in a matter-of-fact way. It is taken for granted like the weather, for which Bunyan has an un-British neglect.

Of course, for pilgrims prayer should be a normal, integral part of everyday living, not just slotted in night and morning. Between busy tasks we need to '"swing back" to attending God and to his presence within us and around us.'[3] Sir Liquat Ali Khan, at one time Prime Minister of Pakistan, recollects asking Lord Halifax where he had disappeared to one day. To his surprise Halifax said he had been communing with his Maker, and had now made up his mind.[4]

The impression *Pilgrim's Progress* gives us of the Christian life is of activity. Whilst the prayerful, reflective side of the Christian is utterly necessary, it is secondary to the outward, mission side. Those who become interested in spirituality for the sake of self-improvement or to find peace of mind misunderstand the gospel. True, there may be an initial phase, as Bunyan himself experienced, when a person seeking the faith is chiefly concerned with personal life and salvation, and energies go into sorting things out and getting order and peace instead of confusion, but this should give way to the main work, the service of God and neighbour.

1. PP pp 45f.
2. For this exposition I have relied on G W Bromiley, *Theological Dictionary of The New Testament.*
3. *A Touch of God,* (ed M Boulding and P Jebb) p 6.
4. R A Butler, *The Art of Memory,* p 30.

18. DELECTABLE MOUNTAINS

The Future

Pilgrims of all times need goals and incentives, and so Christian is taken to the top of the Palace to get a sight of the way ahead and he sees the Delectable Mountains. Never having seen a mountain, Bunyan has to rely upon his fertile imagination, fed by the prophecies of Isaiah. What he describes has the exotic splendour of an Indian painting.

> Behold at a great distance he saw a most pleasant Mountainous Country, beautified with Woods, Vinyards, Fruits of all sorts; Flowers also, with Springs and Fountains, very delectable to behold.[1]

In passing we should be glad to observe Bunyan's pleasure in nature, of which this is but one example. In this he resembles Jesus himself. Bunyan's appreciation of 'light, air, fragrant flowers and open windows,' says Vera Brittain, 'was as far in advance of his time as his views of baptism.'[2] Such a pity she omitted birds for they receive most of his praise. His love for the countryside was doubtless heightened by years languishing in gaol, just as living with concrete and tarmac makes us pine for green spaces.

However, let us leap over a few stages in the journey to see what the pilgrims found when they reached the Delectable Mountains. Only a sentence about the countryside! What interests Bunyan is the Shepherds who entertain folk lavishly. And it is in their names that we find the clue to the identity of these Mountains in the Christian life. They are Knowledge, Experience, Watchful and Sincere.[3] Add them together and one perceives it is Christian maturity that is the goal.

Ask present-day Christians what they would reckon to be the four chief signs of maturity in a disciple and then put them alongside Bunyan's. One would expect to see modern people putting forward love and faith, taking sincerity for granted and rarely mentioning the need to guard against sin. Perhaps the old Calvinist view lacked humanism but ours lacks realism.

Spiritual maturity in itself is not, in Bunyan's eyes, a sufficient inducement to pilgrims. To it has to be added the kind of life it brings, that of peace and security. This is, of course, allegorically expressed, and so when Christian and Hopeful reach the Mountains they drink, wash, eat bunches of grapes and after talking with the Shepherds spend the night in their tents.[4] Mr Great-heart's party is treated to 'a Feast of things easy of digestion, and that were pleasant to the Palate, and nourishing', before taking their rest, each in 'his proper place'.[5]

The invalid food is needed by the 'Feeble and Weak' in the party: Feeble-mind, Ready-to-halt, Dispondencie and his daughter, Much-afraid. Bunyan is at pains to show that the goal is attainable by those with frail faith, not simply those whose faith is as robust as Abraham's.

Pilgrims ramble the Mountains seeing the sights and even attempt to glimpse the Celestial City, *the* goal, through a telescope. Christian and Hopeful's hands trembled yet 'they thought they saw something like the Gate, and also some of the Glory of the place'.[6]

What is important for us to realise is that the Delectable Mountains represent a state within our grasp, this side of death, not diffused in mists beyond it. In Baxter's words, 'it is a life of love, and joy and cheerful progress to eternal joy that he requireth of you, and no more fear or grief than is necessary to separate you from sin.'[7] It is the kind of state reflected by Jesus in his 'Consider the lilies' teaching of *Matthew 6.25ff,* and is a base for positive witness.

1.PP p 45.
2. V Brittain, *In the Steps of John Bunyan,* p 154.
3. PP p 98.
4. Ibid. NB: In Part I they have tents; in Part II a Palace.
5. PP p 238.
6. PP p 100.
7. R Baxter, *Christian Directory,* II p 142.

19. HE THAT IS DOWN

Humility

The feelings of exultation which are commonly felt at the time of publicly confessing the faith and committing oneself to Christ often give way to disillusion and disappointment afterwards when life settles back into the old rut, old sins reappear, and at last an acquaintance finds amusement in taunting one with the hoary charge of hypocrisy.

With this in mind, Bunyan describes a landscape which sites the Church at the crown of a great hill overlooking the Valley of Humiliation into which all pilgrims must descend. Christian slips over a few times, despite the guidance of four virtuous women, Discretion, Piety, Charity and Prudence. 'As it was difficult coming up,' he observes, 'it is *dangerous* going down.'[1]

Bunyan is more conscious of his pastoral role when he writes the second part of his story and he labours to allay pilgrims' fears. Mr Great-heart assures them that they 'need not be so afraid of this Valley, for there is nothing to hurt us'.[2] Bunyan's approach is like Julian of Norwich's: 'If we never fell we should never know how weak and pitiable we are in ourselves. Nor should we fully know the wonderful love of our Maker.'[3]

Mr Great-heart goes on to extol the delights of the Valley, which, contrary to popular opinion, is 'the best and most fruitful piece of Ground', much loved by our Lord, who 'formerly had his *Countrey-House*' there. He commends it for contemplation, being far from 'the Noise and from the hurrying of Life'.[4] (And that in seventeenth century England!)

Humility is the Cinderella of the virtues. Probably this is due to the impact of the ancient monastic ideal of humility engendered originally by the Rule of St Benedict. This Rule is worth our attention and respect but with regard to humility its objective is the submission of the monk's individuality to his community and in particular to his prior who stands in the place of Christ. The monk who climbs to the top of the twelve-runged ladder of humility 'whether sitting, walking or standing should always have his head bowed, his eyes fixed on the ground, and should at every moment be considering his guilt for his sins.'[5]

This brand of humility, passivity, will not do for most of us, buying and selling, raising children, arguing with the bureaucracy. Jesus did not practise it; only in his last hours did he submit as the Lamb of God.

The heart of biblical humility is found in *Romans 12. 3ff,* 'Do not be conceited or think too highly of yourself; but think your way to a sober estimate . . .' Discover what your gift is and set to work with it for the good of all. Paul makes it sound so simple, rational and painless, but it never is.

As Richard Baxter says, we are very ready to 'speak meanly and humbly' about ourselves in general, but are defensive when it comes to admitting specific sins. That is too painful, too shameful. How hard it is to accept that one is not a particularly choice ear of corn in the Lord's field; and harder still to realise that one is only one of many millions.

One sure sign of humility is contentment. Sidney Smith's friends were surprised at his reaction when he was banished from London society to a tiny Somerset village. He had enjoyed a fashionable reputation as a sharp and witty commentator on affairs and had been mentioned for a bishopric. He told them, 'If it be my lot to crawl, I will crawl contentedly.'

Bunyan's own experience in the Valley bore fruit in one of his best hymns, that of the merry shepherd boy:

> He that is down, needs fear no fall,
> He that is low, no Pride:
> He that is humble, ever shall
> Have God to be his Guide.

I am content with what I have,
Little be it, or much:
And, Lord, Contentment still I crave,
Because thou savest such.[7]

1. PP p 46.
2. PP p 196.
3. *Enfolded in Love,* tr members of the Julian Shrine.
4. PP p 197.
5. *The Rule of St Benedict,* tr D Parry, Chapter VII.
6. *The Cure of Church Divisions,* Orme, *Works* p 358.
7. PP p 197.

20. APOLLYON

Self-Confidence

Once down the Valley of Humiliation, Christian is confronted with Apollyon and has the worst, yet most glorious and famous battle of his life. Apollyon is obviously related to the dragon St George is used to slaying in the Mummers' village dramas. He is 'cloathed with scales like a Fish', has 'Wings like a Dragon, feet like a Bear, and out of his belly came Fire and Smoak, and his mouth was as the mouth of a Lion'.

Like the serpent in Eden, he is both intelligent and articulate, and so he and Christian dispute, and it is this that gives us the clue to the true nature of the encounter.

First of all Apollyon lays claim to Christian, 'thou art one of my subjects', and demands to know, 'How it is then that thou hast run away from thy King?' Christian contends that he now belongs to another, 'the King of Princes', and cannot return to the fiend. Then Apollyon reminds him that there was a time when he had given himself to him, and he tries to coax him to return. Christian will not listen and boldly retorts that he much prefers Christ: 'I like his Service, his wages, his Servants, his Government, his Company, and Countrey better than thine, and I will follow him.' Apollyon gently bids him cool down a little and remember what sufferings are in store for Christ's servants, often shameful deaths, and declares that whereas Christ 'never came yet from the place where he is, to deliver any that served him out of our hands,' he has delivered 'either by power or fraud' those who have faithfully served him. Christian remains unmoved, placing his hope in the Coming of Christ in glory.

Apollyon tries a new, more deadly attack. He accuses him of unfaithfulness and asks him how then he can expect any reward. For a moment Christian seems taken by surprise: 'Wherein, O *Apollyon,* have I been unfaithful to him?' The fiend reels off a list of his misdeeds and concludes with a most penetrating thrust: 'and when thou talkest of thy Journey, and of what thou has heard, and seen, thou art inwardly desirous of vainglory in all that thou sayest or doest.' Christian is far from dismayed. 'All this is true, and much more,' he admits, 'but the Prince whom I serve and honour, is merciful.' Having confessed his sins and been sorry for them, he has 'obtained pardon' of the Prince.

Apollyon screams, 'I am an enemy of this Prince; I hate his Person, his Laws, and People.' So ends parleying and battle ensues. It lasts half a day; and half a page! Darts fly, the sword glints; there is roaring and yelling, sighing and groaning. At last Christian is pinned under the fiend and is being slowly crushed to death; his sword has flown out of his hand. In this desperate state Christian manages to find his sword again (God's Word) and he puts the fiend to flight with two thrusts. One is a text from *Micah,* 'Rejoice not against me, O mine Enemy! when I fall I shall arise,' and the other from *Romans 8,* 'Nay, in all these things we are more than Conquerors through him that loved us.'[1]

Strip off the decorative wallpaper and what do we find? What is the real encounter? Is it not the disciple's crisis of self-confidence? Apollyon's terrifying thrust was at Christian's pride in himself as a pilgrim. Falling down in the Valley of Humiliation had hurt him sorely. What a poor example he sets others! His self-confidence drains away as he wakes up to the fact that he is a failure as a Christian, despite his fine name. He only recovers when he puts his trust in God's promises and learns to base his new self-confidence in God's love for him.

Christian rightly praises God for the victory. The church, however, remembered his own courage and erected a monument with this inscription, 'The Man so bravely play'd the Man.' The victory could not be won without God, nor yet without the man. The Guide likened him to Hercules.[2]

It is interesting that nobody else in *Pilgrim's Progress* is attacked by the fiend. But then, they were humble folk.

1. PP pp 47ff.
2. PP p 199.

21. THE VALLEY OF THE SHADOW

Fear

Although most of us have no experience of minding sheep and no desire to acquire it, *Psalm 23* continues to retain a special place in our hearts, and no verse is more valued than the fourth, about the valley of the shadow of death. (In Hebrew it is in fact only gloom, not death). Indeed, we find here a prescription for faith in the time of fear.

In this narrow valley Bunyan allows his imagination full rein. To one side of the path is a deep ditch and to the other a bottomless bog. Further along there are pits, holes and shelvings whilst the path itself is full of snares, traps and nets. To add to his misfortune Christian ventures here on a very dark night. Ghostly beings swish past him uttering chilling, doleful cries. The chief landmark of the valley is the mouth of hell which belches like a volcano. The path runs so close to it that pilgrims are enveloped in smoke and flames, and sparks dance among them. Unhappily morning heralds no respite. Now Christian can plainly see the Hobgoblins, Satyrs and Dragons that infest the pit. At the end of the valley he surveys the 'blood, bones, ashes and mangled bodies' of pilgrims slaughtered by two Giants who live there, Pope and Pagan. And for good measure, when Christiana's party picks its way through this chamber of horrors Bunyan has thought of some fresh terrors to put on display, including Giant Maull, whose speciality is spoiling young pilgrims with 'Sophistry'.[1]

Commentators, then, are right to state that Bunyan's concern here was to protect Christians from doctrinal error. In particular, rationalism was beginning to take the heart out of many a Presbyterian or Anglican Christian whilst Quakerism was pulling the other way and making fanatics. It is sad that reason and feeling have been so often torn apart in the history of the Church. It is still happening.

In this fearful valley some pilgrims, like Bunyan himself, become victims of wrangling voices inside them. This phenomenon is seldom mentioned but is dealt with by Nels Ferré who points out that 'God can use auto-suggestion'.

The real worry, he says, is to be able to distinguish good voices from bad.[2] It was blasphemy, however, which most troubled Bunyan. For example, when people began praising God, he says, 'some most horrible blasphemous thought or other would bolt out of my heart against him'.[3] Too many Christians have suffered needless misery through misunderstanding the nature of the sin against the Holy Spirit.[4] It is far more serious than the thoughtless discharge of foul language against God. It is to despise goodness, truth and love, to abandon oneself wholeheartedly to evil, to disdain forgiveness and thus become unredeemable.

Down in the valley Christian learnt to 'put up his Sword, and betake himself to the weapon called *All-Prayer.*' Christiana's party also 'cryed and prayed' and God sent them 'light and deliverance'. The importance of prayer in the time of stress is not overlooked.

It is rare to be given a glimpse of the 'secret place' in a person's life, particularly that of a public person. But in Lord Stockton's *At the End of the Day,* he relates how he 'went to tell D' (Dorothy, his wife) the good news of the Test Ban Treaty (1963) and 'burst into tears. I had prayed hard for this night after night.'[5]

Bunyan is wise enough not to expect all pilgrims to have the same kind of experience in the valley. Faithful passes through on a bright, sunny day, with no trouble. But Mr Fearing has to be dragged through by Great-heart. 'The Hobgoblins will have me,' he keeps crying. Yet the valley is silent and the pastor believes the Lord has commanded it to be so.

Strange as the scene is that Bunyan paints, it truly conveys what we feel in the valley of gloom and fear. So, in de Caussade's words, 'Come then, past the perils and monsters, guided and upheld by that sure unseen hand.'[6]

1. PP pp 50ff and 197ff.
2. *Strengthening the Spiritual Life,* pp 34f.
3. *Grace Abounding* para 101.
4. Matthew 12:13f.
5. *Op. cit.* p 487.
6. *Sacrament of the Present Moment,* p 41.

22. LOVINGLY TOGETHER

Friendship

"Ho, ho!" called Christian, spotting Faithful ahead of him. He put on such a turn of speed that he couldn't stop when he reached him and went sprawling. 'Faithful came up to help him,' and then 'they went very lovingly on together.'[1]

Friendship is one of the bright colours that cheers the pages of *Pilgrim's Progress*. They say Bunyan was a friendly soul. Certainly Christian is; moreover, Bunyan's pilgrims resemble a jolly party on a tour, friends together, though their journey is to the Kingdom of Heaven. Some people speak derisively of the social club climate of many churches. Yet without it a church would be cold and uninviting. Mere sociability, of course, is about as near to friendship as veneer to solid wood. The pilgrims share together the common concerns of the Kingdom.

It is when trouble hits someone that true friendship shows its strength. Dr Johnson's club used to meet every Tuesday at seven, at The Turk's Head, where it enjoyed food for the stomach and the intellect. Famous men belonged: Burke, Garrick, Goldsmith, Reynolds and others, including Boswell. The depth of their commitment to each other appeared when Johnson's health began to fail and they arranged, with the help of the Lord Chancellor, for him to take a trip to Italy. "This is taking prodigious pains about man," exclaimed Johnson, with tears in his eyes. "God bless you all, for Jesus Christ's sake."[2] At the other extreme it can be dangerous to be without friends when you need them. Simone Weil's contribution to the spiritual dimension of life was tragically cut short because she was alone in London, under-eating, over-working for the liberation of France, and consequently falling ill with TB, which led to her death. Even one friend might have saved her.

There are friends, and there are close friends 'to whom you may impart griefs, joys, fears, hopes, suspicions, counsels, and whatsoever lieth upon the heart to oppress it.'[3] Christian found in Faithful and later in Hopeful such bosom friends. Intimacy like this we know to be therapeutic. It does one good when one can share another's problems: it takes the mind off one's own, and makes their size diminish.

It seems that Faithful and Christian were of an age. Hopeful, however, was younger; perhaps Christian was a father-in God to him. There often are opportunities for older Christians to groom younger ones and perhaps they are not taken up as often as they might be. Excuse a personal reference. When I was a candidate for the ministry, still in my teens, I had to preach a trial sermon and my examiner was an eighty-year-old minister, William Timms. I asked him for his comments and he invited me home to supper and there began one of the richest friendships of my life. We met every week to talk about the affairs of the Kingdom and one night went on talking till dawn. There was an air-raid on at the time.

Is friendship on the decline in our impersonal age? How many there are who find satisfaction in the companionship of a dog or cat. The Christian psychiatrist Frank Lake thinks people in our schizoid world are avoiding close relationships, afraid of feelings. He is perhaps misguided by seeing so many inadequate people, or is he right?

One who has no friends to walk with lovingly can never follow the Lord, nor lay down his life for them, not even a small part of it. Love must be atrophied.

1. PP p 55.
2. James Boswell, *Life of Samuel Johnson*, 1784. Johnson died before the trip could take place.
3. Francis Bacon, *Essays* XXVII.

23. FAITHFUL (I)

Sexuality

Not least among the great revolutions which have taken place in this century is that to do with sex. It would be ridiculous to expect someone living over three hundred years ago to provide us with answers to our pressing problems. What is striking, however, is that Bunyan decided to treat the subject of sex at all, whereas in the contemporary Church there are still too many taboos. Bunyan would not allow spirituality and sexuality to be kept apart in separate compartments from which they inevitably escape from time to time to turn the soul into chaos.

In the course of discussion one day Faithful owned that 'One whose name was Wanton' had tempted him. 'What a flattering tongue she had: she lay at me hard to turn aside with her, promising me all manner of content.'[1] He had not given way, however, and Christian exclaimed, 'Thank God you escaped her.' Faithful replied laconically, 'Nay, I know not whether I did wholly escape her.' It was not long afterwards that he had met 'the Old Man,' Adam, who promised him all three of his daughters in marriage if he would serve him. Their names were 'The lust of the flesh, the lust of the eyes, and the pride of life.' He dallied and then put Adam behind him for good.

In Part II we return to the subject when one of Bunyan's best character studies is introduced, Madame Bubble, who plagues Mr Stand-fast. We see her successors adorning modern magazines and films. She is blasée, after a 'good time' and a gullible man. Great-heart called her a witch and a bold, impudent slut.

> She always laugheth Poor Pilgrims to scorn, but highly commends the Rich. If there be one cunning to get Mony in a place, she will speak well of him, from House to House. She loveth Banqueting and Feasting . . . She has given it out in some places, that she is a Goddess, and therefore some do Worship her.[2]

To Stand-fast she offered 'her Body, her Purse and her Bed'. Repulsed over and again, she returned, smiling and exclaiming, 'I am the Mistress of the World, and men are made happy by me.' Earnest prayer plus the appearance of Great-heart eventually drove her off.

Throughout, it is important to note that Bunyan never shared the disparagement of sexuality so often found in Church history. But he wants us to be fully alert to its abuse and danger.

Surely many disastrous marriages, not to mention love affairs, would not have happened had the parties been aware of the fire they were playing with, and how painful it is to get burnt. Many wander along as if in a dream, only to wake up to the cold truth when it is too late. Alan Paton recounts how he and one of his students fell in love. The friendship deepened. 'I could have stopped it, but I did not.' His wife, however, noticed what was happening and asked him what he was going to do about it and he said, 'Stop it.' He did, and she said, 'What did I do wrong?' The incident seems to have led to the deepening of their relationship.[3]

St Francis de Sales in his instructions to Madame de Charmoisy, who was married to a courtier of the Duke of Savoy, warned her of the way innocent friendships can become sensual and destructive. Glances and embraces can be happy and innocent, but she must watch against 'lingering glances, sensual caresses, long sighs, murmurs about not being loved . . . the solicitation of kisses and other improper attentions.' 'Turn a deaf ear . . . to the snake-charmer's music,' he tells her.[4]

Temptation is unavoidable but falling is not, and Bunyan by mentioning prayer and sharing one's problem with a wise counsellor shows the path to safety.

1. PP pp 57f.
2. PP p 253.
3. *Kontakion for You Departed,* p 97.
4. *Introduction to the Devout Life,* III p 20.

24. A WORD AND A BLOW

Discipline

Faithful next told Christian what happened to him as he climbed the Hill Difficulty.

> I looked behind me, and saw one coming up after me, swift as the wind; . . . he was but a word and a blow: for down he knockt me, and laid me for dead. But when I was a little come to my self again, I asked him wherefore he served me so? He said, Because of my secret inclining to *Adam the first;* and with that, he strook me another deadly blow on the brest, and beat me down backward; so I lay at his foot as dead as before.[1]

After yet another battering, 'one came by, and bid him forbear'. Christian wanted to know who it was. 'I did not know him at first,' replied Faithful, 'but as he went by, I perceived the holes in his hands, and his side: then I concluded that he was our Lord.'

Christian quickly identified the swift man who was 'but a word and a blow' as Moses, who 'spareth none'.

In reality this scene must have taken place in Faithful's conscience, and yet his sense of an external power sent by God to discipline him in love was also real. Our forefathers accepted without question the need to live under authority, to respect and fear it, whether of God or man; and self-discipline like Faithful's was a necessary part of the larger orderliness.

Three centuries ago order was maintained with a severity hard for us to appreciate. It comes as something of a shock to hear a gentle girl like Mercie remark of three bodies seen hanging by the highway, "Let them hang and their Names Rot."[2] In fact Faithful's punishment was mild in a day of ferocious beating and flogging. Even members of dissenting congregations expected to be tried and cut off if they got into sinful ways such as drunkenness, adultery or not attending worship. The Church Book of Bunyan's own congregation testifies to this.

The pendulum has swung to the opposite extreme. According to William Rees-Mogg, past editor of *The Times,* 'the reigning terror of the twentieth century is the rejection of the idea of external discipline.' He held Freud, Spock and Keynes largely responsible.[3]

Laxity has infiltrated the Church, even the religious communities. But there are signs of hope. Richard Foster is one who fights to restore the good name of discipline.[4] As yet the emphasis is very much upon self-discipline, which is more acceptable in this day than obedience to outside authority. However, it should be asked whether self-discipline can take root and flourish in the absence of respect for authority generally.

Slackness is observable in church life. On the part of many who attend services there is unwillingness to accept responsibilities, whilst those who do, seem to expect it to be taken for granted that their other interests will have priority. John Macquarrie is not alone in thinking that the decline of discipline is probably due to indifference.[5]

The idea is abroad that Jesus came to banish fear. That is a half-truth, for he also said, "I will warn you whom to fear: fear him who . . . has authority to cast into hell. Believe me, he is the one to fear."[6] Without fear, as Luther said, we fall into the evil ways of security.[7] And now we find the security cracking under our feet. We have to ask ourselves whether we understand that reverence means recognising authority and being godfearing. Acknowledging God as our Father implies being under his discipline.[8]

1. PP p 58.
2. PP p 177.
3. Robert Moss, *The Collapse of Democracy*, p 78.
4. *Celebration of Discipline.*
5. *A Dictionary of Ethics*, p 90.
6. Luke 12:5.
7. Gordon Rupp, *The Righteousness of God*, p 178.
8. Deuteronomy 8:5.

25. DISCOURSE

Meeting and Talking

> Faith. *Friend, whither away? Are you going to the Heavenly Countrey?*
>
> *Talk.* I am going to that same place.
>
> Faith. *That is well: Then I hope we may have your good company.*
>
> *Talk.* With a very good will, will I be your companion.
>
> Faith. *Come on then, and let us go together, and let us spend our time in discoursing of things that are profitable.*[1]

Nothing pleases pilgrims more than meeting folk on the road and talking with them.

One hears people complaining today that television is killing conversation in the home. If this is so it is worrying because it means that children are getting less training in listening, thinking and expressing themselves, as well as less fun together.

Television, however, is not the only culprit; there are several others. Psychology has shown us that feelings in the end play a greater part than reason. Education has pushed chalk and talk out of the classroom in favour of experiential methods. History tells us that actions speak louder than words; and so does our personal experience. Whereas our Victorian fathers believed that human beings were fundamentally rational beings and that democratic debate would usher in a new era, we are profoundly cynical about words. Conversation in such circumstances was bound to suffer.

By now the harvest of our cynicism about words ripens and the fruit is scrubby. A generation is growing up unable to pay attention to the spoken word. And how does that augur for communication in the future? In public places, in the House of Commons, for example, debate is rare and both words and statistics are used as ammunition to hurt the other side. Confrontation, lobbying and pressurising are the order of the day. Reasoning is futile. Ultimately, frustrated enthusiasts take to violence.

Even churches become prone to the same disease and thoughtful and sometimes poetic hymns must give way to repetitious choruses chanted like manthras, maximising emotion and minimising thought. Prayers and Scripture readings are cut to the barest possible in some congregations, for fear that people will get bored. Such is the fruit of rejecting the marriage of reason and feeling.

In his day Richard Baxter complained about Christians who thought the less reason was used the stronger faith would become, but 'faith is no unreasonable thing' he argued. Certainly the evidence of the Gospels is that Jesus, the Teacher, expected his hearers to use their minds. It was in fact rather hazardous to put a question to him since you were likely to get a poser in return! Intelligence and speech distinguish us from animals. Our powers of reflection, reasoning, projection and creativity reveal that we are made in the image of God. These powers need cultivating.

God has given us Christians no other means of fighting for the Kingdom save his words. Example alone cannot achieve the end. We cut the ground from under our feet when we join in the debasing of reason and talking.

Constructive discoursing begins with our paying attention and listening with interest to the other person, showing we believe in the value of conversation. Only so does one know where to try to lead. An old instruction merits remembering when wishing to convey your view as a Christian: 'Of five things have a care: To whom you speak, of whom you speak, and how and when and where.'

1. PP p 62.

26. TALKATIVE

The Head and the Heart

The trouble with Talkative was not as one would suppose, verbosity – in fact Faithful was his equal in that regard – but his insincerity. His religion was all talk. Christian summed him up as a tall fellow, 'pretty' at a distance, but less pleasing the closer one got. 'His house,' declared Christian, who knew him well, 'is as empty of Religion, *as the white of an Egg is of savour.'* Unreasonable with servants, untrustworthy in business and a devil at home, Christian kept clear of him.

Faithful, however was for some time captivated. 'I was so fond of his company at first,' he told Christian, 'but I am as sick of it now. What shall we do to be rid of him?'[1]

A plot was laid. Faithful was to get discussion going on the power of religion, that is, its effect on someone, and then discover 'whether the thing be set up in his heart.' 'You shall find,' promised Christian, 'that he will soon be sick of your Company too, except God shall touch his heart and turn it.'

Discussion began and Talkative said the first effect of God's grace in the heart was to cause *'a great outcry against sin'.* This was far from satisfying Faithful who cried out, 'Nay hold.' The soul must 'abhor its sin' surely?

'Why, what difference is there between crying out against sin, and abhorring it?' retorted Talkative.

'Oh! a great deal,' replied Faithful, who went on to explain that it is one thing to condemn sin and another to loathe it, particularly in oneself.

Talkative then said that the grace of God gives one '*Great knowledge of Gospel Mysteries',* to which Faithful quickly replied employing every biblical text he could think of to show that knowing is useless unless it leads to doing. Faithful pressed his argument home so hard that Talkative bade him adieu, calling him peevish, melancholy and judgmental.

Talkative is such a caricature that we cannot imagine his cap fitting any of us. Nevertheless, those of us who have to concentrate on thinking, speaking and writing as well as all who love a discussion, have to keep a special watch lest we neglect what Bunyan calls the 'Soul of religion — the practick part'. There is also the danger described by Henri Nouwen of getting 'entangled in such a complex network of discussions, debates and arguments about God and "God issues" that a simple conversation with God or a simple presence to God has become impossible'.[2] Too great a preoccupation with books may set one in the same bracket as Talkative. Luther remarked that some become 'learned with the multiplication of books, but most unlearned Christians'.[3] Talkative's hat suddenly fits the swollen head.

No one is advocating that Christians need not bother to know what their faith is about. Luther wrote books and was no stranger to the most serious debates. Faithful is to be commended for his thoroughgoing grasp of theology and his courage in taking on a formidable-looking debater. Christians are often far too afraid to try. William Neil Connor, 'Cassandra', was well-known for his skill in argument. Victims said it was like being spun into a combine harvester to argue with him. You were 'cut, baled and bounced out into the wilderness'. Dr Billy Graham asked to meet him. Connor expected a fanatic and found a good and gentle man. 'Goodness and simplicity are a couple of tough customers,' he commented. 'I never thought that friendliness had such a sharp cutting edge. I never thought simplicity could cudgel us sinners so damned hard.'[4] It was not the doctor's knowledge or experience so much as his directness, 'truth in love', which Connor felt.

1. PP pp 62-70.
2. *The Way of the Heart,* p 47.
3. Gordon Rupp, *The Righteousness of God,* p 172.
4. Robert Connor, *Cassandra,* pp 148, 142f.

27. EVANGELIST

Spiritual Guidance

> *Faithful* chanced to cast his eye back, and espied one coming after them, and he knew him. Oh! said *Faithful* to his Brother, who comes yonder? Then *Christian* looked, and said, It is my good friend *Evangelist.* Ai, and my good friend too, said *Faithful*; for 'twas he that set me the way to the Gate.[1]

Greeting one another as old friends do, Christian recalled Evangelist's 'ancient kindness and unwearied laboring' for his good. Observe what Evangelist then asks them, in particular his last question: 'How hath it fared with you, my friends, since the time of our last parting? *what* have you met with, and *how* have you behaved yourselves?'

Evangelist, then, is a 'father confessor' to pilgrims, not simply one who proclaims the Gospel, not only a director and corrector of faults, nor yet a prophet who must warn them of trials in store. Spiritual guides have played an essential part in most religions, including Christianity. Until the early part of the nineteenth century pastors of most Baptist and Independent churches were expected to undertake this role, backed up by the discipline of the church meetings. When liberalism swept across Protestantism each person was expected to look after his own soul. It became a private matter. Today, even Roman Catholics find their confessional much in decline.

At last fresh shoots are rising from the old stock. Among those who have contributed in varying ways one remembers Evelyn Underhill, Leslie Weatherhead, Paul Tournier and Dietrich Bonhöffer. Now we have the pastoral counselling movement. The style is very different from the old, laying stress on helping, healing, guiding. It is a pity that it tends to be thought of as appropriate for people with 'problems' rather than good for everyone. Perhaps essential?

> A minister is not only for Publike Preaching, but to be

a known Counsellor for their souls, as a Lawyer is for their estates, and the Physician for their bodies.[2]

So said Richard Baxter over three hundred years ago. How is it, then, that today Christians who run to the doctor over the most minor ailments, never suffer from spiritual disorders, and never need to consult with those who have a wider and deeper understanding of such things than themselves? It is lamentably easy to be confused about one's own affairs. The wood cannot be seen for the trees. My will and God's will start spinning round one another until I cannot tell which is which. I become a bad judge of my own affairs. One lesson Arthur Wellesley, later Duke of Wellington, learnt marching up and down the Iberian Peninsula was that men love to live by illusions. He mistrusted the judgment of every man, he said, where his own wishes were involved.[3] We are really quite incompetent to manage ourselves by ourselves.

However, not all ministers are gifted spiritual guides. Baxter admitted that some Christians have to put up with 'a very weak minister.' Today this should not be the problem it was. It is widely accepted now that anyone seeking spiritual help should be free to choose a guide and, moreover, to change guides when necessary. Bunyan chose wrongly at first. When he was sorely troubled, fearing that he had committed the unforgivable sin against the Holy Spirit, he consulted an old, experienced Christian. This person heard him out and agreed, 'he thought so too.' 'I had but cold comfort,' says Bunyan. However, he thought he would question him further and this revealed that although he was 'a good man', he was 'a stranger to much combat with the devil'. Bunyan did not lose heart. He sought a better counsellor.[4]

The chief value, however, of talking to a spiritual guide of one's choice, someone whose lips are for ever sealed, is in the relief the soul finds in sharing a trouble, a feeling of guilt, a fear, an anxiety, a problem, getting it off one's chest. He who does it walks away, not only with fresh insight and wisdom, but with a much lighter step, rejoicing that Christ has again shown forgiveness. There is but one proviso: to be open. 'Be sure you deal sincerely, and cheat not yourselves by deceiving your counsellor, and hiding your case. To do so by your lawyer, is the way to lose your suit.'[5]

1. PP p 70.
2. *The Reformed Pastor,* p 82.
3. Arthur Bryant, *The Years of Victory,* p 355.
4. *Grace Abounding to the Chief of Sinners,* para 180.
5. Baxter, *Christian Directory,* Orme II p 117.

28. VANITY FAIR

Witness

Like Christian and Faithful, step cautiously into Vanity Fair. It is old and big, open every day, and here you may get anything you want, property and preferment, pleasures and precious stones, even sordid items like blood and bodies. Whores, Masters and servants jostle. There's juggling and drama. But watch out: thieves, murderers and adulterers abound. In fact, here we have all the ingredients of our friend, the television, save that we would have to add for good measure, drink, drugs, sex, hooliganism and terrorism.

The sight of two pilgrims in puritan garb caused a hubbub and some cried, Fools. The pilgrims tried to shut out the noise putting their fingers in their ears, and they looked upwards 'signifying that their Trade and Traffick was in Heaven'. One stall-holder accosted them, 'What will ye buy?' and 'They, looking gravely upon him, said '*We buy the Truth.*'[1]

Here then is the issue, one of values: vanity *versus* truth. The point being made is that worldly values prove false; they fail to yield the satisfaction they promise. Worldliness often slides into immorality and criminality. Its bent is destructive and its end is the rubbish-tip of the cosmos. Christian values, in contrast, are sound and bring peace and contentment. A witness at Faithful's trial alleged that he had heard him say that Christianity and the customs of their town were diametrically opposite and irreconcilable.

But is life black and white like this? Understandably, the life of Restoration England seemed rotten to a sectary confined to a foul gaol for a long time. What is questionable is the way Bunyan seems to relish the persecution. Jesus did not exalt over his; what the authorities were doing to him filled him with pity for them. Bunyan seems tainted with the heresy the Early Church fought called Donatism. The Donatists 'witnessed to the faith by penance and suffering and aspired finally to a martyr's death. There was no salvation outside this body of the elect.'[2]

Unless we withdraw from normal life like members of the religious orders, we have to work out for ourselves a life-style which is a witness to the values we believe in. We do not take vows of poverty, chastity and obedience, but we are dedicated to disciplining our financial and sexual activities and submitting our motivation to the will of God. On the one hand it means self-denial yet on the other it means single-mindedness. If it sounds to some a wretched, nerve-wracking business, this is not so because awareness of the goodness of God transforms the whole of life into something sacred and good. As Bonar says in a well-loved hymn:

> Praise in the common things of life,
>   Its goings out and in;
> Praise in each duty and each deed,
>   However small and mean.

What a shame it is that we have forgotten Luther's teaching that any of us can hear the calling of God in ordinary everyday life, for everywhere service is involved.

Witness includes words. Actions speak louder than words, we say, and yet they only speak louder if there are words. Christians can explain modestly why they find the faith attractive. They can show how through Christ they have come to terms with their life and found hope in God.

They have to witness in public and social affairs. Bunyan, sitting in gaol, cannot be expected to take much interest in such things. Those of us who are at liberty are called to do so in the tradition of the Hebrew Prophets. Dag Hammarskjøld once made a pessimistic jotting: 'The madman shouted in the market-place. No one stopped to answer him. Thus it was confirmed that his theses were incontrovertible.'[3] Perhaps he was recalling Hitler's rantings. 'A handful of just and honest men,' said Martin Buber, 'can prevent a society from becoming corrupt.'[4]

1. PP pp 72ff.
2. W H C Frend, *The Rise of Christianity*, p 654.
3. *Markings*, p 137.
4. Audrey Hodes, *Martin Buber*, p 39.

29. FAITHFUL II

Sacrifice

The pilgrims were arrested for causing a civil disturbance. Faithful's trial constitutes the most dramatic and satirical passage in *Pilgrim's Progress.*

The witnesses for the prosecution are Envy, Superstition and Pickthank, and the Judge is Hate-good, perhaps modelled on Lord Chief Justice Jeffries or else on Sir John Kelynge, who conducted Bunyan's court appearance. Neither of them was in the least afraid of showing bias. Hate-good shouted at Faithful when the evidence against him was concluded, 'Thou Runagade, Heretick, and Traitor!' Faithful would not be put down easily.

> *May I speak a few words in my own defence?*
> *Judg.* Sirrah, Sirrah, thou deservest to live no longer, but to be slain immediately upon the place; yet that men may see our gentleness towards thee, let us hear what thou hast to say.[1]

Faithful did his best to rebut the accusations. 'Then went the Jury out.' In naming the jurors Bunyan's fertile imagination, once employed in gaining him a reputation for prowess in blasphemy and now converted, blossoms. There are Messrs Blind-man, No-good, Malice, Love-lust, Live-loose, Heady, High-mind, Enmity, Lyar, Cruelty, Hate-light and Implacable, and they condemn Faithful to death, crying out, 'hang him, hang him,' though Cruelty shrieked, 'hanging is too good for him!' He was taken out to be scourged, lanced with knives, stoned, pricked with swords and burned at the stake. The author is guilty of sensationalism at this point. Dissenters were never treated so despicably but Bunyan wanted to remind readers of the martyrs Foxe had immortalised.

Christians and others are suffering persecution in far too many parts of the world. The afflictions of prisoners, like the miseries of the poor and hungry in the third world and the iniquitous and growing disparity between the rich and the poor everywhere, are troubles that some Christians and even some congregations try to forget. They behave like Rat in *The Wind in the Willows,* who, when Mole asked him what was beyond the Wild Wood, replied,

> Beyond the Wild Wood comes the Wide World and that's something that doesn't matter, either to you or me. I've never been there, and I'm never going, nor you either, if you've got any sense at all. Don't ever refer to it again, please.[2]

Something not so dissimilar has been heard at the church door after the preacher had 'talked too much' about South Africa.

As the years pass by and human rights are largely ignored by some governments, one is tempted to wonder if our concern is of any use. But prayers, petitions and letters, plus monitoring of course, do affect victims and also authorities. People are less likely to vanish without trace. Post for prisoners may not reach them but it tells the authorities that they are not forgotten. And somehow the message gets through and the knowledge that the outside world remembers them and prays for them gives them comfort and hope.

To pray for the victims of injustice is good but to pray meaningfully for persons is even better. Take, for instance, Anna Chertkova, a reformed Baptist, declared 'criminally insane' and sentenced to indefinite confinement in a special psychiatric hospital in 1976. An eye-witness described her situation in 1979:

> If you talk too much you get an injection of sulphazin . . . Anna got sulphazin because she does not believe in Communism but openly believes in God. They put her with atheists who tear up the Gospel. She is not allowed to talk to the patients about God; they threaten her with isolation, and say she is an enemy of the people.[3]

The prisoner's fear is of giving way under pressure. 'There is only one thing I dread,' said Dostoievski, 'not to be worthy of my sufferings.'[4] Paul cannot be accused of the lack of courage, yet he called on fellow Christians to pray for him that he might be bold for Christ whilst in chains. Those of us who are free owe it to those who are not to keep on remembering them.

1. PP p 78.
2. *Op cit* by Kenneth Grahame Chap 1.
3. Keston College, *The Right to Believe*, 1986 No 3.
4. Quoted by Victor Frankl, *Man's Search for Meaning*, p 66.

30. BY-ENDS

Example

Bunyan does not like us asking awkward questions. We must not ask, for example, how Christian escaped from prison in Vanity Fair. The only answer he provides is elusive: it was the work of him 'that over-rules all things'. However, escape he does, and is soon joined by a young fellow, Hopeful, one attracted to him by the example of the two pilgrims at Vanity Fair. But we soon pass from good examples to a bad one and this is By-ends. The name is obsolescent now. Had Bunyan been writing today he might have chosen Underhand, Compromise or even Mole, a name suggesting someone whose example undermines all the Church stands for.

With a little imagination, as Bunyan unfolds the character and background of By-ends, with his host of friends, one can make out the same ugly faces and fat forms, finely clad, which crowd many a Hogarth print: Lords Turn-about, Time-server and Fair-speech, Messrs Smooth-man, Facing-bothways and Two-tongues, who is Parson of the Parish; and in a corner deep in discussion as to the defence of a case of Simony, are Hold-the-world, Mony-love and Save-all. With not a little pride, By-ends recounts his rise up the social ladder:

> To tell you the truth, I am become a Gentleman of Good Quality; yet my Great-Great-Grandfather was but a Water-man, looking one way and Rowing another.[1]

He is not afraid to add that he got most of his wealth 'by the same occupation'. Subtle! His wife now takes her place in our picture. She is none less than 'Lady Faining's daughter', 'arrived to such a pitch of Breeding, that she knows how to carry it to all, even to Prince and Peasant.'

The charming and courteous clique in the town of Fair Speech are pillars of the Church. Religion for them is the way to peace and prosperity. Abraham and Solomon are their patron Saints.

Christian, whose creator knew all about persecution, feels bound to remonstrate with By-ends. Disciples have to be prepared to go against wind and tide. They must own

Religion in rags as well as in Silver Slippers, and 'stand by him too, when bound in Irons as well as when he walketh the Streets with applause.'[2]

By-ends and company find the pilgrims too narrow-minded for them: they 'judge and condemn all but themselves.' By-ends leaves them with disdain, claiming the right to his own opinions; his principles are 'harmless and profitable'.

The seventeenth century, convulsed by revolutions and civil wars, was a time of judgment for Christians. You had to decide openly at the critical moment whether to take up the cross or not. Issues are not so sharply contrasted in peaceful times like our own. Nevertheless, minor decisions can be symptomatic, revealing the priorities of heart and mind. We hear a variety of excuses, sport, family visits, decorating, for cutting attendance at worship. They say something about our priorities, perhaps reminding the conscience of Jesus' tale of the Great Feast and the feeble excuses made by guests who, being preoccupied with their personal affairs, stayed away.

Not a few who frequent services, hear sermons and take communion, want the best of all worlds. They resemble the settlers that Shalmaneser placed in Samaria whom *Kings* tells us 'feared the Lord', but 'also served their own gods'.[3] Elements of idolatry lurk in most of us who have confessed Christ as Lord. Richard Baxter is worth quoting:

> It is his pleasure, his profit and his honour, that is the natural man's trinity, and his carnal self that is these in unity. Indeed, it is the flesh that is the principal idol.[4]

It is an idol which repeatedly haunts us, turning up unexpectedly when we supposed we had banished it for good.

The last we hear of By-ends is a rumour that he fell into the Silver Mine on the Hill Lucre and that would not be surprising.

1. PP p 81.
2. PP p 82.
3. II Kings 17:33.
4. *The Saints Everlasting Rest*, Orme, Wks XXII p 183.

31. HOPEFUL I

Forgiveness

At length the pilgrims came to a pleasant river where they enjoyed a well-earned holiday, eating, drinking and sleeping among the lilies under trees endowed with medicinal properties. To set out on their travels again was hard. Moreover, 'the way from the river was rough.' However, there appeared to be a better way through a meadow leading in the same direction. Hopeful felt hesitant about it but Christian quickly brushed his cautiousness aside and the two crossed a stile into the field and set out, following another pilgrim some way ahead of them. All went well until night fell, it was dark, and they heard the pilgrim crash down into a great pit. They hurried to the place and called to him but only heard a few moans and then — silence. Then they knew the worst. They had gone wrong.

> Hope. *I was afraid on't at very first, and therefore gave you that gentle caution. I would have spoken plainer, but that you are older than I.*
> *Chr.* Good Brother be not offended, I am sorry I have brought thee out of the way, and that I have put thee into such eminent danger; pray my Brother forgive me, I did not do it of an evil intent.
> Hope. *Be comforted my Brother, for I forgive thee;* and I believe too, that this shall be for our good.[1]

This episode is one of the small gems of *Pilgrim's Progress.* It is a joy to discover it because forgiveness, strange to say, is not given the prominence by Christians that it received from our Lord. It is like Cinderella over against gratitude and kindness, save that these cannot be described as ugly sisters. 'The discussion of forgiveness in the literature of Christian theology and ethics is conspicuously light,' says Paul Lehmann.[2] Seeing its importance in Christ's parables and in his prayer, not to mention the cross itself, it is something of a mystery why it is neglected.

This lack of teaching leaves people thinking of forgiveness as an occasional unpleasant duty when they must confess their guilt to their heavenly Judge, or worse still to an unheavenly human being, or else listen to some wretch stammering out words of self-condemnation, and having to say, 'Alright but don't do it again!' We are dominated by secular notions of crime and punishment instead of heavenly grace, reconciliation and healing.

Forgiveness has its genesis in our lives wherever we happen to be, at home, on the road, in school, shop or office, with simple things. This is why Jesus taught us to pray about it daily. Forgiveness is as necessary as food for life to go on smoothly. It lubricates like oil. Upsets caused by misunderstandings or omissions, thoughtlessness or stupidity, all have to be excused and made good. All day long we have to be 'living sacrifices'. This is spiritual life.

This simple daily training should prepare us for the less frequent but far more painful and serious ruptures in relationships which are bound to occur. 'God has thus ordered things that we may learn to bear one another's burdens; for there is no man without his faults, none without his burden.'[3]

One day in 1947 Corrie ten Boom had been preaching on forgiveness and had mentioned that she had been a prisoner at Ravensbruck Concentration Camp, when she suddenly recognised to her great consternation a man who had been a guard there, and a particularly cruel one. He approached her openly declaring, 'I was a guard there.' He said he had undergone conversion and knew God had forgiven him, but now he pleaded for her forgiveness. She was put to the test. The gospel obliged her to put out her hand in a gesture of forgiveness but her feelings did not go out. Then, to her amazement, as their hands were grasped, she felt a current of healing warmth run through her arm.[4]

1. PP p 92.
2. *A Dictionary of Christian Ethics* (ed J Macquarrie), p 131.
3. Thomas A Kempis, *The Imitation of Christ,* 1, 16.
4. *Tramp for the Lord,* pp 58ff.

32. DOUBTING CASTLE

Despair

The two pilgrims escaped the pit but could not find their way back through the darkness to the stile, and early next morning were caught in the grip of Giant Despair who cast them in the dungeon of Doubting Castle, to languish without food, drink or light. The author's sense of fun projects an unlikely giant, henpecked by his wife Diffidence and dependent on her instructions as to how to treat the prisoners. In bed each night they consulted and she decided the tactics. Her name, Diffidence, incidentally, has no connection with modesty; it describes the fearful paralysis and hopeless gloom she produces in other people. So, the first morning the giant, armed with a crab-tree cudgel, gave the pilgrims a dreadful beating.[1]

What caused Christian most anguish was the fact that he, an older Christian, a responsible leader, had led a young man astray, into misery. The forgiveness of his brother and his heavenly Father failed to raise his spirit because his own pride prevented him forgiving himself. This is a common enough weakness in Christian people. *Real* humility accepts our human limitations and, as St Bernard says, 'is not surprised at imperfection, even at sin, whereas the proud man is astonished when he commits a fault, and because he is proud he cannot forgive himself any blemish.'[2]

Over-confidence, self-righteousness and spiritual pride, the common temptations of middle-aged, successful people, were well enough known to John Bunyan.[3] And they lead to a black hole. His spiritual diagnosis is paralleled by St Teresa who says that aridity is often due to lack of humility and obedience (what happened at the stile).[4]

In this situation God seemed to have abandoned them and the Devil poured icy doubts over them. What these were we are not told, but elsewhere Bunyan speaks of the doubts that had assailed him. Many sound quite modern. The worst was questioning 'the being of God and the truth of his

Gospel'. Another time he wondered if the Scriptures 'were not rather a fable'. He was troubled by other faiths for 'Every one doth think his own religion rightest.' As a preacher who dearly loved the Bible, it was frightening to find it sometimes no better than 'a dry stick' and one's own heart 'so dead'. Once when he was depressed, he was asked to preach to a crowd of prisoners but he felt so 'empty, spiritless and barren' that he doubted whether he could utter 'so much as five words of truth with life and evidence'.[5] Like Cervantes' Don Quixote at a critical stage, the almost demented Christian wonders if this pilgrimage isn't after all nothing but a figment of the imagination.

Dark times like this are far from uncommon. Eventually the endless thumbing over questions has to stop. 'There is no remedy to this darkness but to sink into it,' remarks de Caussade,[6] and St John of the Cross promises that if we know how to remain quiet, without a care, without a struggle or effort, our fatigued spirit will 'delicately experience the interior nourishment'.[7]

The next plan of the wicked pair was to suggest suicide to their prisoners. It is noticeable that it was Hopeful who argued with Christian against it. What he says is familiar enough. Suicide is against the commandment not to commit murder, and furthermore, who can be sure that the grave brings peace — 'hast thou forgotten Hell?' It is surprising to see no reference made to the effect of suicide upon one's family. Suicide notes often show that people assume that their relatives will be glad to be rid of them, but it does not work that way. Those left feel guilty and depressed, blaming themselves for failing to give sufficient love and support to the one in need.

To add to their misery, the next day the Giant shows them the skulls and bones of previous prisoners, surely a reference to the sad, perplexing fact that so many good comrades on the way quit the Church and we seldom know why.

How did it all end? The prisoners pray as never before, all

one Saturday night, and just before dawn Christian cried, 'What a fool am I . . . I have a *Key* in my bosom, called *Promise,*' and so, trusting in the promises of God, the two escape.

1. PP pp 93ff.
2. Quoted by Thomas Merton, *The Silent Life,* p 85.
3. Vera Brittain, *In the Steps of John Bunyan,* p 312.
4. *The Interior Castle,* see Third Mansions.
5. *Grace Abounding,* paras 96-97. Concl 1. 1,4.
6. *Sacrament of the Present,* p 33.
7. *The Dark Night of the Soul (tr Kavanaugh and Rodriguez),* p 315.

33. HOPEFUL II

Frankness and Prudence

After a stop at the Delectable Mountains they headed for the dangerous Enchanted Ground. Christian told the tale of Little-faith who met with three rogues, all brothers. The first, Faint-heart, demanded Little-faith's purse, while the second, Mistrust, helped himself to a bag of silver in his pocket, and then the third, Guilt, struck him on the head with a club and 'fell'd him flat to the ground.' Being disturbed, they fled, leaving poor Little-faith to 'scrabble on his way.'[1]

Hopeful wanted to know if Little-faith wasn't glad the rogues did not get his jewels. After all, he might have needed them in bad times to pawn or sell. Christian rounded on him. Was he in his right mind? Who would buy the jewels (ie one's saving faith)? In any case how would he gain admittance to the heavenly city without them?

'Why art thou so tart . . . ?' protested Hopeful. Taking no notice, Christian went on to lecture his young colleague.

'I acknowledge it,' admitted the other, *'but yet your severe reflection had almost made me angry.'*

A few more rude remarks from Christian, and Hopeful returned to the attack. Why didn't Little-faith stand up to the rascals? They were cowards and would have left him alone. This made Christian quite cross. It was alright to say that with hindsight, but in the same situation Hopeful would have given in after a blow or two. Happily the conversation moved to a more amiable level.

Team-mates and friends, husbands and wives are not going to see eye-to-eye all the while, no matter how dedicated to Christ and to peace they may be. The sad exceptions are those where one person dominates the other. Jesus had differences with Peter, and Peter with Paul, and Paul with Barnabas, these two splitting up and going different ways.

A prudent person keeps silence as long as possible but

there comes a time to speak out. It is always a somewhat risky business, like walking a narrow cliff path in a gale. Scripture counsels us to have regard for gentleness and love in speaking the truth; it does not guarantee that we shall be received by an ear that will listen. If we are heard, we may get a bruising reply, or else the hearer may just vanish into the night without a word like Judas.

Prayer is the finest preparation for frank speaking. Yet the most damaging exchanges are those which take place without warning, leaving one exposed. The more prayerful our life, however, the more likely it is that the relationships and issues, not forgetting our own feelings, will have been subjected to examination in the divine presence and thus the ground prepared in advance of any eruption. Nevertheless a contretemps will hardly surprise us. Where relationships are sound, cordial and open, where mutual respect and trust exist, with no hint of deception, there is no reason to expect that a dispute will lead to rupture. Our Lord's rebuke to Peter, 'Away with you, Satan, you think as men think, not as God thinks,' did not break their love and loyalty.[2]

There are awkward times, however, when prudence compels one not to be frank. We may know something that others are not entitled to know. Worse still, it may be our duty, like Rahab, to put others off the scent. Francis Bacon observes that diplomats and statesmen in particular face this kind of work, though it can come to any of us, and he says Christians must have a clear conscience in such cases. Anyone with a troubled conscience will be unmasked by his enemies.[3]

Christian went on to caution Hopeful on the subject of discretion and valour. He tells his young companion that it is not prudent always to confront the muggers. Christian had fought his way out of danger when he had to, but he doesn't court it. 'For such footmen as thee and I are, let us never desire to meet with an enemy, nor vaunt as if we could do better when we hear of others that they have been foiled, nor be tickled at the thoughts of our own manhood.'

1. PP pp 102ff.
2. Mark 8:33.
3. *Essays*, VI.

34. ENCHANTED GROUND

Complacency

> I saw then in my dream, that they went till they came into a certain Countrey, whose Air naturally tended to make one drowsie, if he came a stranger into it. And here *Hopeful* began to be very dull and heavy of sleep, wherefore he said unto Christian, I do now begin to grow so drowsie, that I can scarcely hold up mine eyes; let us lie down here and take one Nap.

'By no means,' Christian sternly replied. This was what the Shepherds of the Delectable Mountains had warned them against.

'Two are better than one,' remarked Hopeful, feeling grateful for his fellow's diligence.

Christian thought that they should ward off slumber by talking together and suggested that Hopeful begin by relating how he came to be a pilgrim.

> When Saints do sleepy grow, let them come hither,
> And hear how these two Pilgrims talk together.

It was certainly effective in keeping Hopeful awake and also provided points for discussion, until a third person, Ignorance, came upon the scene.[1]

Who has never been to the Enchanted Ground? When, after long years of struggle, one has mastered one's trade or profession and some success attends it, if marriage is secure and children growing up, and around is a circle of good friends, surely a sense of satisfaction is legitimate. But if it be fondled and hugged it turns to smugness. The same happens to churches where numbers are good, activities flourish, the books balance, and to cap all, there is a proud record of giving to charities abroad and at home.

To make matters worse, the more successful and eminent, the more flatterers are attracted like moths to a bright light at night. Jesus, only too well aware of this, issued the warning, 'Alas for you when all men speak well of you; just so did their fathers treat the false prophets.'[2] Just the same, Christian and Hopeful were lured away by the Flatterer on the borders of the Enchanted Ground and caught in his net.

Flattery is indeed a net. It gives you an image which you then feel you must live up to. Suppose you are praised for being so very busy. If you fall for the flattery you will end up on a tread-mill. Or perhaps your image is of being a Good Samaritan here, there and everywhere. For fear of spoiling that image you may allow your own home to be neglected. To fall in love with the image others fix on you indicates spiritual slumber.

In fact churches organise discussions, conferences, group meetings and the like with the same motive as Christian had in mind: to wake up nodding pilgrims and exercise the obese. Unfortunately there are always the loners who refuse to take part. Ignorance was one of these. 'I take my pleasure in walking alone,' he declared. What the discussion into which he was dragged revealed was the depths of his ignorance and complacency. Of vital truths he had no idea whilst being firmly attached to illusions. All he wanted was to be left undisturbed in his ignorance.

Besides discussion there is prayer. Prayer is usually badly affected by complacency as trees are by drought. If, however, a pilgrim arrives at the Enchanted Ground with a vigorous prayer life, complacency will be kept at bay. Mr Stand-fast was such a pilgrim and was found there upon his knees. Complacency often creeps upon us when life consists largely of routine, presenting little challenge, and the remedy is to train ourselves to reflect upon God whenever we have a moment to spare. 'If not actively concerned with some business or person, we should "swing back" (like a door with a spring) to attending to God and to his presence within us and around us.'[3]

Finally complacency is not simply sleeping; it is dreaming that all is well. If the Apostle confessed that he was still pressing on towards the goal, surely we need to. The famous accompanist, Gerald Moore, told mediocre musicians that they needed to write out a hundred times a day, 'It is not easy.' That could be said to us as Christians. Moore continued, 'To the Toscaninies, Solomons, Fischer-Dieskaus, nothing is easy; and the further they progress, the deeper they probe, the more experience they imbibe – the harder they find the going and the less they are satisfied.'[4]

1. PP pp 111ff.
2. Luke 6:26.
3. Dom Philip Jebb in *A Touch of God* (ed M Boulding), p 6.
4. *Am I Too Loud?*

35. I SAW THE LORD JESUS

Theophany

Strictly speaking, theophany is impossible. 'No man has ever seen God,' says *John (1.18),* for 'God is spirit' *(4.24).* Nevertheless this has never inhibited people from having visions. Jesus himself saw 'the heavens torn apart and the Spirit, like a dove, descending upon him.'[1]

In relating the long tale of his conversion, Hopeful came to a remarkable experience. For a long time he had been brooding on his sinfulness and seeking reassurance, and then, one day, when he was feeling 'sader then at any one time in my life' and 'looking for nothing but *Hell,*'

> I saw the Lord Jesus look down from Heaven upon me, and saying, Believe on the Lord Jesus Christ, and thou shalt be saved.
>
> But I replyed, Lord, I am a great, a very great sinner; and he answered, *My grace is sufficient for thee* . . . . Then the water stood in mine eyes . . . .[2]

Bunyan is very careful to preface this passage with Hopeful's words, 'I did *not* see him with my bodily eyes, but with the eyes of mine understanding.' Or should we say imagination?

Christian too had a vision of Christ, as he told Piety, 'I saw one, as I thought in my mind, hang bleeding upon the Tree.' That was when his burden fell from him.[3]

Here Bunyan is relying on his own experience. In *Grace Abounding* he recounts how after seven weeks of miserable doubts concerning his salvation he went one day to a meeting where the text 'My grace is sufficient for thee' was repeated three times. 'It was,' he says, 'as though the Lord Jesus looked down from heaven through the tiles at him.'[4]

Undoubtedly Protestantism has exaggerated the effectiveness of the Word and the mind, and underestimated the power of vision and imagination. Protestants have reacted like Martin Luther, who is said to have thrown an ink-pot at a vision of Christ to dispose of it – successfully. But Bunyan took such phenomena seriously. He knew that a vision or a voice might change the whole direction of someone's life.

Ernest Payne, the eminent Baptist and Ecumenist, had an intellectual bent. However, as a young student at King's College in the Strand, when he was leaving one evening to go to his chapel's Golden Jubilee celebrations 'he became conscious of a Figure behind him with his hand on his shoulder impelling him forward. He took the figure to be Christ.'[5] From then on Payne knew his calling to the ministry.

But we are moving into a danger area. When St Bernadette in 1858 had visions of the Virgin Mary there ensued 'an epidemic of false visionaries and morbid religiosity'. Indeed, this hindered the establishment of Lourdes. St Teresa of Avila, well-known for her ecstatic experiences, especially the time when she felt a spear of divine love had pierced her heart, warned people about the peril of desiring unusual religious experiences.[6]

Nevertheless, ordinary people feel in touch with God more often than is recognised. Morton Kelsey described his experiences in four categories which, to his surprise, he found other people shared. They were (i) a vague presence, (ii) a burning reality bringing relief, (iii) wisdom offering guidance, and (iv) the giver of joy and fulfilment.[7] The writer has, in the course of pastoral work, again and again come across people who have confided that they had had similar experiences 'out of the blue' which had led them to take special action.

Bunyan admits, however, that his golden hours were few and far between. It is, after all, routine walking with God that matters most, and to that subject we next turn.

1. Mark 1:10.
2. PP pp 116f.
3. PP p 40.
4. *Op. cit.* paras 205ff.
5. W M S West, *To be a Pilgrim,* p 15.
6. D Attwater. *Dictionary of Saints,* pp 62, 308f.
7. *The Other Side of Silence,* pp 10ff.

36. FALLING AWAY

Spiritual Exercise

The relation between falling away from discipleship and spiritual exercises, such as praying and reading Scripture, is that the latter can be tapped and scrutinised like a barometer to tell us whether the spiritual outlook for the disciple is going to be Fair or Stormy, whether indeed falling away is round the corner. 'They that wait upon the Lord shall renew their strength,' said Isaiah; conversely, those that fail to, are going to remain faint and weary, and are likely to fall.[1]

In *Pilgrim's Progress* these matters are discussed by Hopeful and Christian, though in typical seventeenth century style. Hopeful with his firstly, secondly, thirdly, fourthly on why people fall away, and Christian describing the nine steps down which they go until they are 'hardened'. It is all too prolonged and elaborate for us to go into, but both pilgrims agree that backsliders cannot have been truly converted in the first place. With hindsight it is easy to say this; it is another matter before the slide begins. Can any Christian afford not to learn to recognise when spiritual health is deteriorating?

The barometer is falling when we neglect to pray, put it off or hurry it. Not wanting to pray can end up not being able to.

Praying and versing oneself in Scripture constitute a discipline which must be worked at. It is no different from other worthwhile activities in this respect, e g athletics or music. A serious effort has to be made to set aside time. For most of us it means short devotions normally, with longer periods as often as possible. That every day should begin and end with prayers and praise is an ancient and honoured tradition and there is evidence of it in *Pilgrim's Progress,* but for greater spiritual profit longer, more leisurely sessions must be encouraged.

First, however, we should ask what we are doing it for. It is not to recharge spiritual batteries; nor for self-improvement, although benefits of such a kind are valued by-products. The object is to attend upon God, both as his servant and friend, to bring offerings of loving worship, to listen carefully to his Word and to commune with him with the mind and heart in prayer. The order is important. Begin by being still and at rest, at attention like a soldier awaiting a command. No running into the Father's presence like a child from school full of news and troubles.

We are all different and no one pattern of devotion is suitable for all. Each has to persevere, trying this and that, until the right diet is established, and even then it may be necessary to change it if you get stuck fast in a rut.

Prayers should include praise, adoration, thanksgiving, confession of sin, intercessions for others, petitions for our own affairs, dedication. Hymns and psalms aid concentration and most people find that a mixture of written prayers and one's own extempore ones is helpful. Intercession is often hard work. What shall we pray about and what shall we ask for? It is surprising too how often one forgets very important matters. There is also a tendency to say too much, as though God needed information in our possession or else he might get things wrong! Yet when all is said and done, what Mother Julian says remains true:

> It gives more praise to God and more delight if we pray steadfast in love, trusting in his goodness, clinging to him by grace, than if we ask for everything our thoughts can name.[2]

Sometimes we cannot put into words what we feel and our spirit communes with his in silent prayer.

There are many aids to regular Bible reading and these are invaluable, but useless unless the reader will spend a while thinking prayerfully about the passages, ie meditating. Sometimes a few words will attach themselves to you — this is called the bouquet or button-hole. Of course, other devotional books may also be read. Why not keep a note-book with prayers, texts and thoughts for future use?

Daily devotion is a rhythm, like the heartbeat, keeping us in spiritual health and strength.

1. Isaiah 40:30f.
2. *Enfolded in Love,* p 5.

37. MR GREAT-HEART

Ministry

What do we expect of pastors and preachers? What qualities do they need? Bunyan's response to these questions is found in Mr Great-heart, the minister.

He is beloved of the pilgrims for his affectionate care. On one occasion he brings them gifts of wine and fruit to refresh them. With the weak and faint-hearted he takes infinite pains. Yet above all, it is his valour which is outstanding.

He resembles a champion in a medieval tale, for there is nothing he likes better than to confront a giant, fell him and chop off his head! His is the same spirit that inspired Don Quixote, save that his adversaries do not turn out to be windmills but the real fears of pilgrims. For example, the fear of persecution which anyone had to face who inclined towards joining a dissenting congregation appears as Giant Grim, who, along with two lions, bars the way to the Palace Beautiful. He is slain, as also are Giant Despair and Giant Slay-good, from whose clutches Mr Feeble-mind is rescued. The abiding message seems to be that the pastor can liberate anyone from the bondage of fear, providing the pilgrim 'keeps Heart-whole towards his master'.[1]

With Giant Maull Great-heart has his worst combat. Early on he is beaten down on his knee and he nearly has his skull broken. The 'breath came out of the Giant's nostrils, as the heat doth out of a boiling Caldron.' At last Great-heart pierces the giant under the fifth rib and he faints.[2] Commentators debate whether Maull represents Romanism or Rationalism; what is sure is that it is what Blake calls 'mental fight' which the minister finds hardest.

In *The Ministry of the Word* Charles Browne calls on preachers to be fearless in their thinking so as to be truthful and humble in their speaking,and never to dread error. The timid preacher loses his message behind carefully balanced views. Then there is the preacher who can be observed making 'excessive speed over unmade roads', who is skimming over his own unresolved conflicts. Browne also admonishes preachers to put life first, not doctrine. 'The minister of the Word is called to be an expert in living rather than an expert in doctrine.' Doctrine should help people to have life more abundantly.[3]

Here the dangers loom up. Someone thinks that honour is given to truth by hanging one's doubts over the pulpit, much to the distress of the congregation. Another, unable to face painful thinking, is happy to offer people confectionery instead of real bread. Sadder still is the preacher whose testimony lacks conviction. *Southern Mail* by Antoine de Saint-Exupéry, one of the best novels of our century, contains the visit of Bernis to Notre Dame in Paris where he hears a powerful preacher on 'Come to me'. Christ is the answer to the world's needs, is the theme, yet all the preacher conveys to Bernis is empty despair under brave words. 'What I heard was no act of faith, only an utterly desperate cry.'[4]

If we want better preaching and counselling there has got to be a sea change. Ministers today are expected to be busy — organising activities, festivals, work in the community. Time to read, meditate and pray flickers out. The cost is burn-out. 'Behind the smooth word, the smiling face, and the polite handshake . . . is a frozen anger, an anger which settles into a biting resentment and slowly paralyses a generous heart,' says Henri Nouwen in *The Way of the Heart.* Let us learn from the Desert Fathers. St Antony, 'the father of monks', discovered that it was in solitude, confronting his own demons and learning to lean upon his Lord, that he came to understand the hearts and moods of people, and thus could 'offer insight, comfort and consolation.'[5] We need to take to heart *Acts 6.1-4* and decide *who* is to do *what.* Do we want to have ministers who are brave enough to fight principalities and powers or not?

1. PP p 223.
2. PP pp 202ff.
3. PP pp 44-47.
4. PP pp 66ff.
5. PP pp 24, 33.

38. MR FEARING AND CO

Compassion

Not all pilgrims are laudable, like Faithful and Hopeful, Christiana and Mercy, old Honest, Mr Standfast and Mr Valiant-for-truth: many are 'improbable saints' — 'the young, the old, the infirm, the despondent, the tiresomely scrupulous, the fearful and the anxious'. Christian himself is hardly heroic: 'left to his own devices, Christian never would have achieved the quest, and yet, quite against the odds, he does achieve it.' The lesson is that 'any man may, through grace, become a Christian hero.'[1]

One of the most difficult pilgrims was Mr Fearing, uncle of Mr Feeble-mind — both had a 'whitely Look' — who froze every other step of the way. Though he had the root of the matter in him, as Mr Honest said, and was never in danger of turning back, he suffered from chronic pessimism. Great-heart said he had 'a *Slow of Dispond* in his mind, a *Slow* that he carried everywhere with him.' He made no fuss about the Hill Difficulty; he had no fear of the lions of persecution; Vanity Fair did not bother him; his doubts were about his own worthiness to be Christ's. Thus his life was a burden to himself and he was troublesome to others. Great-heart said he only knew how to play the bass. When Honest asked the pastor how he put up with him, he replied: 'I did so, but I could very well bear it; for Men of my Calling are often times intrusted with the Conduct of such as he was'. 'My master, you must know, is one of tender Bowels, especially to them that are afraid,' and in fact his journey was made as easy as possible for him and when he came to the River at last, where he was sure he would drown, never had the water been so low, and he crossed 'not much above wet-shod'.

Christiana's contribution to the discussion of Mr Fearing is particularly notable. 'I thought no body had been like me,' she says, 'but I see there was some Semblance 'twixt this good man and I, only we differed in two things'. She kept her troubles to herself; his 'brake out.' Also, his troubles stopped him knocking at 'the Houses provided for Entertainment' whereas hers made her knock the louder.[2]

Others too need help. Feeble-mind had to be carried up

the Hill Difficulty and Little-faith required constant nursing after being mugged by Guilt. The fellowship kept before it the task to 'encourage the faint-hearted, help the weak, be patient with them all'.[3]

We meet all sorts and conditions and call them friends in the Church. It is no place to be proud but to mix with simple folk.[4] One of the Desert Fathers, Abbot Arsenius, a renowned Greek and Latin scholar, surprised colleagues by taking counsel of an old uneducated Egyptian. He told them, 'I have indeed apprehended the learning of the Greeks and Latins, as this world goes: but the alphabet of this countryman I have not yet been able to learn.'[5] 'Men and women of gravely divergent views and vastly different backgrounds,' says Norman Goodall, have 'to think differently about and care more for, the kind of people of whom they would otherwise have only an impersonal knowledge or whom they would meet only on a plane where the deepest encounters between person and person never take place.' Some of these encounters, he adds, were costly to him, 'accompanied by much tension of mind and stress of spirit'.[6]

One of our faults is that we judge too often by worldly standards. One of the saddest confessions found in literature is that of Lady Baden-Powell who admits that not until her son was dead did she come to appreciate him.

> Poor Peter. I wish I had understood him better. I had been so completely devoted to and admiring of my brilliant husband that I did not make sufficient allowance for our son. He had always been such a disappointment to me, yet he could not help it . . . It was almost as if I was impatient with him for not being as outstanding as his father.

Peter died and tribute after tribute arrived speaking of his friendship, gentleness and concern for others. 'Too late I realised that, in the things that really matter, Peter *was* his father's son after all.'[7]

1. N H Keeble PP pp xvii.
2. PP pp 207-11.
3. 1 Thessalonians 6:14.
4. Romans 12:16.
5. Helen Waddell, *The Desert Fathers,* p 117.
6. *One Man's Testimony,* pp 71f.
7. *Window on my Heart,* pp 232f.

39. GET SUPPER READY

Hospitality

No one can read *Pilgrim's Progress* from end to end without sensing that besides wind and weather, lions and giants, hobgoblins and foul fiends, and labours night and day, a warm glow of companionship keeps surging up. Thus Christiana and her party find themselves lodging first at an inn kept by Gaius and then at another run by a Cypriot, Mnason, names of New Testament hosts.[1]

A trait of absurdity creeps into the cuisine. The cook Gaius is called 'taste that which is good'. Doubtless Mr Tasty to customers! The menu is derived from the Bible: 'a Heave-shoulder and a Wave-breast', followed by a 'Dish of Milk well crumbled' for the children, 'Butter and Hony' and then apples and nuts, all washed down with 'a Bottle of wine, red as Blood'. 'They drank and were very merry.' In fact, after the boys went to bed, the rest stayed up talking till dawn! They remained at the place for over a month and when they were leaving Gaius prepared another feast, 'and they did eat and drink, and were merry.' At this inn too were the celebrations of family weddings when Christiana's Mathew married Mercie and his brother James married Phebe, the daughter of the Inn-keeper. Christian does not seem to have fared so lavishly on his pilgrimage.

The popular image of a Puritan as a kill-joy is not borne out in fact. Perry Miller says they were undoubtedly too intense for us, searching their souls incessantly, taking themselves so seriously, and yet they had 'a rollicking sense of humour'.[2] Asceticism was foreign to them. Not for them St Thomas à Kempis' morbid attitude to physical things. 'To eat and drink . . . is a real trouble and affliction to the devout man, who would rather be released and delivered from all sin.'[3] The Puritans could not find this in the life and teaching of Jesus and that was good enough for them.

The responsibility for making a success of an hotel or a Christmas party lies with the host or hostess. Gaius, the Inn-keeper, was a model of friendliness and efficiency, running his place like a family *pension,* with no formality. All

Christian homes should be, as is said often enough at marriage services, places where both friends and strangers receive a welcome. A popular subject for Orthodox ikons is derived from *Hebrew 13.2,* 'Remember to show hospitality. There are some who, by so doing, have entertained angels without knowing it.' The pictures show Abraham entertaining three identical angels so arranged as to suggest the Trinity. Hospitality, then, has a spiritual dimension. It may well involve planning, purchasing expeditions, hours of cooking and other preparations, perhaps taking people to see places; it means that a hole is made in one's purse and one's time. It should be a cheerful sacrifice.

Mnason invited friends from the town to meet the pilgrims staying with him. This hospitality is what Christian travellers frequently enjoy as they move about. We have new friends awaiting us in new places. In these days an increasing number of churches are twinned with others abroad and members have the privilege of staying in each other's homes. It is all peace-building.

In Bunyan's time travel was so difficult that relatives and friends used to stay for weeks with one another to make the trouble worthwhile. That does not apply so much today. Hospitality in our time has a new role: to show friendship to lonely, often young, people, away from home, to people of other races or countries who may feel alienated, and to elderly folk, especially widows and widowers, who have to manage alone and sometimes do not look after themselves very well.

The German scholar Adolph von Harnack upbraided his friend Karl Holl for being so miserable, 'turning every fruit tree God gives you into a weeping willow.' 'What is the use of Christianity if it doesn't give us a cheerful countenance . . . ? Shall I add up your possessions — good things, trusted friends, ability to work — so that you are in duty bound to joy and thankfulness? And to spread joy and humour around you . . . '[4] He sums it up.

1. PP pp 215ff, 228f.
2. *The Puritans,* pp 59f.
3. *The Imitation of Christ,* 1. 22.
4. Quoted by Gordon Rupp, *The Sixty-Plus.*

40. MERCIE

Good Works

The emphasis on good works in the modern Church, which sometimes threatens to make the Second Great Commandment into the First, is noticeably absent from *Pilgrim's Progress.* There are several reasons for this. Organised charity was only in its infancy in Bunyan's time and in any case could hardly be expected to occupy much of the thought of a man spending his prime years in gaol. The advent of quick communication and easy travel means that the needs of the world are today far better known. Again, Protestant theology placed the stress on faith, not works. Nevertheless there are important allusions to the need of good works towards the end of the Second Part of *Pilgrim's Progress.*

He paints a pleasing picture of his little Bedford church. 'The *Pilgrims* grew acquainted with many of the good people of the Town, and did them what Service they could.' Mercie was pre-eminent in helping the poor and in return 'their Bellys and Backs blessed her'.[1]

Christians are urged to be generous. On Mount Charity pilgrims are shown a man cutting out coats and garments for the poor from a bundle of cloth which never diminished – 'he that hath a Heart to give of his Labor to the Poor, shall never want withal.'[2] Then there is the old gentleman with a love for riddles who says,

> A man there was, tho some did count him mad,
> The more he cast away, the more he had.

Gaius, the Inn-keeper, guesses this one.

> He that bestows his Goods upon the Poor,
> Shall have as much again, and ten times more.

He explains, 'I have learned of my Lord to be kind, and have found by experience that I have gained thereby.'[3]

Though convinced that works will save no one, Bunyan was equally convinced that words alone were worthless. The Interpreter took pilgrims into his garden to see a tree 'whose *inside* was all rotten, and gone,' and yet 'it grew and had Leaves.' It was to indicate the worthlessness of people who 'with their mouths speak high on behalf of God, but indeed will do nothing for him.'[4] Bunyan's attitude is like Baxter's: 'Christ is so far from redeeming us from a necessity of good works, that he died to restore us to a capacity and ability to perform them.' 'Every day is given you for some good work.'[5]

Of course, it is not 'do-gooding' that is being encouraged for the objective then is to make the doer feel good, no matter whether the recipient does or not. That kind of good work is roundly condemned by Paul in *1 Corinthians 13*. There is no true love in it. Morton Kelsey warns us about caring tasks with egocentric motives: 'We can no longer be emotional children . . . allowing this kind of love to flow through our lives.'[6]

St Frances de Sales is practical in his advice. Everyone should learn what particular work of love he or she can do. Preference should be given to those that show gentleness and kindness, not ostentation.

> Among the servants of God, then, some devote themselves to serving the sick, some to teaching children, some to adorning churches . . . They are like embroiderers working in silk and gold and silver on various backgrounds, weaving countless lovely patterns like so many flowers.[7]

Not all good works are pretty. Palm Sunday should remind us of good works of a different kind, challenges, acts of protest and reform. Bunyan was in prison for such an act. There are many household names in this field, like those of Elizabeth Fry and William Wilberforce, but they are followed by countless unknown people with the fire of the Old Testament eighth-century prophets in their bones. In South Africa and South and Central America and elsewhere Christians are sacrificing themselves in good works of this kind, and they need our support, our prayers. Archbishop Tutu has said, 'Who can win against those who are being prayed for all round the world?'

1. PP p 231.
2 PP p 239.
3. PP p 219.
4. PP p 168.
5. Orme Wks II, *Christian Directory*, pp 322-6.
6. *The Other Side of Silence*, p 65.
7. *Introduction to the Devout Life, III.*

41. HIGHLY FAVOURED

Women and Men

If we were to ask a group of Christians of various denominations to guess who said, 'For as Death and the Curse came into the World by a Woman, so also did Life and Health,' or at least to say whether it was by a Catholic or Protestant, it would be understandable for people to suppose that such praise for Mary must come from a Catholic, probably from one of the great ancient Teachers of the Church. In fact Bunyan put these words into the mouth of Gaius, the Innkeeper. They seem to be strangely inspired by a text in *1 Corinthians 15.21f,* 'For since by man came death, by man came also the resurrection of the dead. For as in Adam all die, even so in Christ shall all be made alive.' Bunyan's lack of academic theological education gave him a freedom which he was not afraid to use. Gaius continued,

> Yea, to shew how much those that came after did abhor the Act of their Mother *(Eve),* this Sex, in the Old Testament, coveted Children, if happily this or that Woman might be the Mother of the Saviour of the World. I will say again, that when the Saviour was come, Women rejoyced in him, before either Man or Angel. I read not that ever any man did give unto Christ so much as one *Groat,* but the Women followed him, and ministred to him of their Substance. 'Twas a Woman that washed his Feet with Tears, and a Woman that anointed his Body to the burial. They were Women that wept when he was going to the Cross; And Women that followed him from the Cross, and that sat by his Sepulcher when he was buried. They were Women that was first with him at his Resurrection *morn,* and Women that brought Tidings first to his Disciples that he was risen from the Dead. Women therefore are highly favoured, and shew by these things that they are sharers with us in the Grace of Life.[1]

Bunyan had good reason to feel indebted to the opposite sex. His second wife, Elizabeth, had been left caring for four step-children, one blind, with only a trickle of income, what charitable friends could offer plus what John could raise by making laces by the gross in his cell. Moreover, she had made valiant efforts to get him released at the time of Charles II's coronation when a number of prisoners were set free. It must have been an ordeal for a young, poor and uneducated woman to journey to the House of Lords with a petition for Lord Barkwood; then she was told to place it before the next County Assizes, which she did without result. Next, she managed to get an audience with the Judges and Justices outside the Court and she dared to argue with them. Towards the end, Sir Thomas Twisden declared Bunyan's doctrine was 'of the Devil'. Elizabeth's final words were, 'When the righteous Judge shall appear, it will be known that his doctrine is not the doctrine of the Devil.' Sir Matthew Hale, later to be Lord Chief Justice, advised her to 'apply thyself to the King, or sue out his pardon, or get a writ of error,' but she didn't; she hadn't the resources.[2]

It is also interesting to note that Bunyan refused to allow a separate prayer meeting for women at the Bedford church. Spiritually men and women are on the same plane. This view has received more support among nonconformists than other denominations. It has taken time for it to affect the organisation, yet women were voting in Church Meetings long before the State enfranchised them. And early in this century the first women were being ordained to the ministry in Congregational churches. Nevertheless, prejudice is not quite dead.

1. PP p 217.
2. See Vera Brittain, *In the Steps of John Bunyan*, pp 213ff, for a fascinating account of this.

42. MUSICK, MUSICK, MUSICK

Arts and Relaxation

The Welsh poet R S Thomas reviled Protestantism as 'the adroit castrator of Art: the bitter negation of song and dance' which 'botched our flesh'. Of song, of music? Never! F W Dillistone is on target when he says, 'Presbyterians and Puritans, Methodists and Evangelical Anglicans throughout their history have been deeply suspicious of colour and costume, action and movement,' both in and out of church, but they managed to satisfy people's emotional needs through singing, music and choral works.[1]

Calvin himself displays the uncertainty and anguish many Protestants felt about music. He taught that it was one of God's gifts intended to 'recreate man and give him pleasure'. He insisted on having singing as part of worship against strong opposition. Music, he said, 'has a great secret and almost incredible virtue to move hearts.' But when his music master planned harmonising psalm-singing, Calvin quarrelled with him and would have none of it, ruling that God only needed 'a pure and simple modulation of the voice'.[2] The problem has always been to decide when Aphrodite begins threatening the Maker of All Things.

In England Dissenters long argued over the role of music, if any, in worship. Bunyan, gifted with a keen ear and pleasant voice, was all for music. No one would stop him. As a craftsman in gaol, he contrived to remove a rail from a stool, hollow it out, pierce it and produce a flute of sorts. He was always composing songs and verses, much of it to amuse and teach children. It is not surprising, then, that the hero of *Pilgrim's Progress* also makes up songs and verses, or that Christiana loves music. One night Mercie hears her laughing in her sleep and in the morning she explains that she heard such joyful music in a dream; Mercie exclaims, 'Wonderful! Musick in the House, Musick in the Heart, and Musick also in Heaven, for joy we are here.'[3]

Puritanism left little room for relaxation. When Bunyan turned to Dissent he was obliged to give up two pastimes he much enjoyed, bell-ringing and dancing. Unconsciously, he continued to love them. A narrower Dissenter would not have imagined the bells ringing out for the pilgrims arriving in heaven. Nor would he have put to paper for the public to read the 'jocund and merrie' scene which followed Mr Great-heart's slaying of 'Gyant Dispair.' Christiana and Mercie struck up a tune on the Viol and Lute and Mr Ready-to-halt took 'Dispondencie's daughter by the hand' and 'to dancing they went in the Road.' Here Bunyan's ever-present sense of the ludicrous takes over: 'True, he could not Dance without one crutch in his hand, but I promise you, he footed it well; also the Girl was to be commended, for she answered to the musick handsomely.'[3]

Pilgrim's Progress shows us how unsuccessful Puritanism was at exorcising the exuberant spirits, even of eminent members of its own party. Puritanism went too far in destroying games and the Arts. On the other hand, they have a way of demanding single-minded worship if they can get it and so threatening their Creator. Chaim Potok's novel, *My Name is Asher Lev* vividly describes the tension experienced by a young Jewish artist as the rival claims of art and Hasid tradition, with standards so utterly diverse, fight for his life and soul.

Hobbies, pastimes, the arts themselves are like food and drink, necessary for our health. But to bow down and worship them, giving them whatever they ask of us, is as bad as living to eat.

1. *The Christian Understanding of Atonement*, p 425.
2. T H L Parker, *John Calvin: A Biography*, pp 87ff.
3. PP p 236.

43. THE LOOKING GLASS

Bible Study

We have reached the last pages of the two parts of *Pilgrim's Progress,* where the narrative wanders sluggishly, like a river in marshlands near the sea. Readers will no doubt have discerned how different the atmosphere is from the wind and weather on the hills and in the valleys of Part I. The allegory too has changed. Whereas in Part I it is easy to recognise, in Part II it often becomes fanciful and sometimes baffling. The Hill Difficulty, for example, needs no explanation; the same cannot be said of Mercie and the Looking-glass.

This stretches the imagination beyond breaking point. Mercie seemed unwell; she feared a miscarriage. It took Christiana to discover the cause. She was pining for the mirror hanging up in the Shepherd's dining room, and was ashamed to ask for it. But Christiana pronounces her desire to be virtuous, for this was no normal glass.

> It would present a man one way, with his own Feature exactly, and turn it but an other way, and it would shew the very Face and Similitude of the Prince of Pilgrims himself . . . Yea such an excellency is there in that Glass, that it will shew him to one where they have a mind to see him; whether living or dead, whether in Earth or Heaven, whether in a State of Humiliation, or in his Exultation, whether coming to Suffer, or coming to Reign.

Mercie was given her glass, her Bible. On top of that, the generous Shepherds, who appear not to have been in the least narrow-minded, presented all the women with necklaces, ear-rings and jewels to wear on their foreheads![1]

Perhaps Mercie was afraid to ask because a Bible was such an expensive article in those days; it is different now. But when it was expensive it got used well. One wonders how many church members are seriously reading the Bible nowadays.

The Catholic Church has no doubts about its role as the

'Church of the Eucharist' but what of Protestants today? 'Their specific gift is to be Churches of the Word,' says Brother Roger, founder of the mixed Catholic-Protestant Taizé Community. He admonishes all Protestants, not simply preachers, to see in Scripture the message God has for them and for society. Whenever he hears Bach's chorales and hymns, he says he is reminded of 'the extent the Word of God was loved, taken seriously' in earlier centuries, 'how it penetrated, disturbed and transformed the Protestant Christian to the very depths of his being.' How much experience have we of God speaking to us through Scripture?[2]

Many Christians seem lacking in purpose in reading the Bible. They amble about in it as if they were at an art exhibition. Mercie knew what she was after: seeing herself and her Lord.

To profit from the Bible, and to enjoy it, besides some background knowledge being useful, it helps to read slowly, sometimes aloud, for the Bible was written for public speaking. Thus the eloquence of Job, the passion of Paul, the rhythm of psalms and the drama of many a dialogue come alive and imagination is kindled. To see, you must imagine. This is the seed-bed of meditation. Now I can see myself — in a haughty Pharisee, a dejected David, a wrathful Jezebel or peevish Martha.

As for seeing Christ in Scripture, what about the Old Testament then? In Bunyan's time people saw in figures such as Moses or Elijah prefigurations of Christ. Biblical scholarship has changed our attitudes. Nevertheless we can still see in the heroes and events of the Old Testament many features which remind us of Christ and the Gospel. *'The whole Bible means one thing,'* says Olive Wyon 'that God alone is, and that he has sent His Son, Jesus Christ, to be the Saviour, King and Judge of all mankind.'[3]

Bunyan's metaphor here may be far-fetched in some ways but his insight into the two-fold motive for studying the Bible, to see God and yourself, is sound.

1. PP pp 240ff.
2. Rex Brico, *Taizé*, p 200.
3. *On the Way*, p 111.

44. THEY TARRIED AND SLEPT

Old Age

The nearest *Pilgrim's Progress* gets to retirement is when the pilgrims reach the country of Beulah, where the birds are singing, the flowers blooming and the sun shining. In fact shining night and day, according to Bunyan! And here the pilgrims enjoy a spell of solace. The gardener invites them into the King's orchards, vineyards and gardens; he also shows them the King's Walks and the Arbors where he delighted to be: 'And here they tarried and slept.'[1]

Retirement as we know it is, of course, a modern invention. Bunyan can be forgiven for hoping for a while to tarry and sleep after all his exertions, though we know that too much of that is detrimental. We would like to invite him to join us today bird-watching, pressing wild flowers, pruning trees in the garden; or perhaps collecting old copper utensils would be enjoyable to the old tinker.

Probably he would prefer to lead us along the King's Walks and develop our spiritual capacities. It is likely that people in the seventeenth century were more aware of the other world than we are and he could tell us about their experience. What he says to whet our appetite is:

> Here they were within sight of the City they were going to: also here met them some of the Inhabitants thereof. For in this Land the shining Ones commonly walked, because it was upon the Borders of Heaven. In this Land also the contract between the Bride and the Bridegroom was renewed.

Are we, individuals or churches, making use of the leisure people now have in retirement to further the spiritual life?

On the whole retired people are more contented than those still absorbed in 'the rat race', and can echo the Shepherd boy's song, 'I am content with what I have.'[2]

What of increasing infirmity? This is only hinted at in Part I. Like Barzillai, who was asked by King David to go up to Jerusalem to live, the time comes when one has to ask to be excused. At eighty, without spectacles, false teeth and a hearing aid, the poor fellow complained, 'I cannot tell good from bad; I cannot taste what I eat or drink; I cannot hear the voices of men and women singing. Why should I be a burden any longer on your majesty?'[3] Even with modern equipment, it is often wise to demur.

Growing old gracefully is no mean achievement. It is as much a spiritual discipline as anything else in life. Innumerable fears poke their wicked tongues out at one. What about decrepitude and pains? What about loneliness day after day, month after month, year by year? How are you going to like losing your independence, your privacy, letting others bath you like a baby? Will you have a stroke and be unable to remember much and become suspicious, accusing people of stealing your underclothes? What humiliation! With Christ, who knows about humiliation, dereliction and our fears, we shall survive and his grace will be sufficient.

There is a collect for Maundy Thursday which reflects our Lord's washing of his disciple's feet.

> Almighty Father,
> whose Son Jesus Christ has taught us
> that what we do for the least of our brethren we also do for him:
> give us the will to be the servants of others as he was the servant of all,
> who gave up his life and died for us,
> yet is alive and reigns with you and the Holy Spirit, one God,
> now and for ever.

It is, then, a spiritual privilege to serve the elderly in their need, for through them we serve our Lord. Yet it is also a privilege, usually unrecognised, to be the recipient of kindnesses which benefit us but are done also for him and to his glory. Without the elderly the world would be a worse, colder, even more pitiless place.

1. PP pp 126f.
2. PP p 197.
3. II Samuel 19:35.

45. NO BRIDGE OVER THE RIVER

Death

A young student nurse burst into tears.

'Ellen's died,' she sobbed, 'and I couldn't do anything.'

'Its the first time its happened to you?' queried the Sister.

The girl nodded.

'It's something we all have to learn to accept,' Sister continued.

Good Friday is the day we have to face the fact of death. Sadly, that is why a number of people stay away from its services. Sad, because Jesus is helping us accept death by his death.

The pilgrims came to the river which 'stood betwixt them and the Gate'. 'There was no Bridge to go over.'

As pilgrims differ in their living, so they do in dying. No two are alike. Hopeful crossed with comparative ease. 'I feel the bottom, and it is good,' he cried. One by one the Post came summoning them and they went confidently, without fuss. Christiana went with dignity and Dispondencie's daughter 'went thorow the River singing, but none could understand what she said.'

When his turn came Ignorance was not worried. He was the type that the psalmist detested:

> For there are no bands in their death:
> but their strength is firm.[1]

He was soon across, the only one to go by boat. The ferryman was Vain-hope, and, sure enough, at the Gate the shining ones bound him hand and foot and took him away.

Strangely, it was Christian who had the worst time. The very thought of the river filled him with despondency. In the river he sank and rose time and again. All his old sins and fears returned and 'apparitions of Hob-goblins and Evil spirits' haunted him. His spirit was clouded with darkness and horror. 'Also here he in great measure lost his senses, so that he could neither remember nor orderly talk . . . ' In lucid moments he revealed that he thought Christ had deserted him. Then, one day, he was seized with the words of Isaiah: 'When thou passest through the waters, I will be with thee, and through the rivers, they shall not overflow thee.'[2]

Bunyan repeatedly stresses that people should prepare themselves for death, practically as well as spiritually. For one thing, they should make a will. Too many pilgrims leave it until the summons comes. In these days of fatal road accidents that is too late. People should consider how they can express gratitude to their relatives and friends. Christiana called Mr Great-heart to her and told him 'how Matters were', and gave him a ring.[3]

Whilst there are pilgrims today who cherish the Christian Hope, many others are not sure what they believe. Curiously, the surest of people are agnostics who are certain death is the end. The fact that none of us can draw a sketch-map of heaven is a great drawback.

Huw Weldon, according to his friend Norman Podhoretz, was one who lived a 'truly godly life.' Like many, he had forsaken the devout and literal faith of his Presbyterian parents, and yet he 'never lost his belief that the reason we are here on earth is to serve God and praise him.'[4] Death, however, he took hard, suffering not only great physical pain but spiritual torment too. Clutching out for peace, he turned to Bach's cantata *Ich habe genug* (I have had enough) but it provided him with no consolation. Because, says the friend, Bach believed in the afterlife and could 'welcome death as a deliverance into the arms of his Saviour.' Perhaps Weldon was not sufficiently prepared.

We shall consider the afterlife further in our last section. What has ever been true is that one's confidence in it is dependent upon the length and depth of one's friendship with Christ crucified, enabling one to have a foretaste in this life of life eternal. Nouwen observes that Buddhists accept death calmly because they live with Nirvana. So can Christians if they live with Christ. The Sacrament of Holy Communion symbolises this truth.

1. Psalm 73:4 (AV).
2. Isaiah 43:2 (AV).
3. PP pp 128f, 132, 257ff.
4. *The Times*, 22nd March 1986.

46. LAY MY BOOK, THY HEAD AND THY HEART TOGETHER[1]

Interpretation

Is life a journey or a pilgrimage?

At first sight *Pilgrim's Progress* may seem a disappointing book on the spiritual life. It does not set out to provide instruction on how to pray, read the Scriptures or practice meditation. Instead, it is about the ordinary life we all live, with its ups and downs, its interesting characters, good and bad, the places we remember affectionately and others we would rather forget. Yet it is also about our reactions, for this everyday life constantly raises problems and crises requiring discernment and decisions; it engenders moods of doubt and despair as well as easy confidence, not always justifiable; it occasions erring and straying, the flesh being so strong. It's about our world too, and what we make of it, full of beauty and destruction, with good friends and men of violence. Ultimately it's about God and the world, about seeking and finding him, immanent in Christ, forgiving and saving.

What *Pilgrim's Progress* should bring home is that life is all of one piece. It is a mistake to try to wrench the spiritual out of the physical and isolate it for then it will dry up and die. Indeed one could say life is a journey and a pilgrimage.

Sometimes the question is asked: whether there might be for ordinary Protestants something comparable to the Catholic religious vows of poverty, chastity and obedience. The answer has to be in the negative because the two life-styles are so different, one being engaged in the world and the other disengaged from it. Indisputable as this is, the questioner may still feel unsatisfied. He or she may be seeking something simple yet profound to guide them amidst the complexities of Scriptural and Church teaching.

There are, may I suggest, three characteristics of the pilgrims, especially evident in Christian himself, which can easily be turned into promises. They are implicit in all exemplary Christian living; they could be explicitly made, either in private or in public.

To be constant.

To be courageous.

To be cheerful.

These are no easier and no less fruitful than the aforementioned vows.

Pilgrims are not distinguished by heroics, simply by their faithfulness and obedience to God, by sheer persistence. They are constant friends and neighbours to those in need; constant in marriage and in duty to their work. They are not distracted by worldly temptations. They endeavour to keep a constant balance between the head and the heart, solitude and society, confidence and humility, faith and work, restraint and refreshment, seriousness and mirth. They are constant at prayer

Who would true Valour see
Let him come hither;
One here will Constant be,
Come Wind, come Weather.
There's no Discouragement,
Shall make him once Relent
His first avow'd Intent,
To be a Pilgrim.[2]

Be courageous, not fearful, is a word that comes across strongly from Bunyan in gaol; it echoes our Lord. In the Valley of the Shadow, at Vanity Fair and supremely fighting Apollyon, facing the self, courage — for Christ is with us.

And to be cheerful, because of God's grace, even after falling. The shepherd boy who sang, 'He that is down needs fear no fall,' was said to live 'a merrier life' and to wear 'more of that Herb called *Hearts-ease* in his bosom, than he that is clad in Silk and Velvet'.[3]

Constancy in clamouring materialistic society is a difficult discipline requiring self-denial. Courage in a world seemingly bent on self-annihilation by one means or another witnesses to great faith. Cheerfulness shows that there are ways of happiness other than resorting to drink, drugs and indulgence. Pilgrimage is to be lived and proclaimed for mankind's sake and God's.

1. PP p 7.
2. PP p 247.
3. PP p 197.

47. THE CHRISTIAN HOPE

Our Easter

On Easter Day we rejoice to hear familiar passages of Scripture and to sing hymns of triumph. Perhaps we listen yet again to a sermon on the empty tomb. The subject attracts preachers as a jam-pot attracts wasps.

We should not forget that Easter is our Easter. This receives ample emphasis in Scripture.

> Praise be to the God and Father of our Lord Jesus Christ, who in his great mercy gave us new birth into a living hope by the resurrection of Jesus Christ from the dead.[1]

Paul speaks of Christ's resurrection as the first fruits and at his return 'in Christ shall all be made alive'.[2] In the best-known Easter hymn, 'Christ the Lord is risen today', Charles Wesley brings the point home in verse 5:

> Soar we now where Christ hath led,
> Following our exalted Head;
> Made like him, like Him we rise:
> Ours the cross, the grave, the skies.

Where has Christ led us? What is this Christian Hope? It will be a daring preacher in these days who will expound on the Holy City. Three centuries ago it was different. Bunyan glories in describing its wonders in detail. The modern reader is likely to dismiss it out-of-hand with a scornful smile. Our problem as Christians is how to convey that heaven is real without using imagery which mocks its spiritual nature. And first of all we have to clear our own minds about it.

> Give me the wings of faith to rise
> Within the veil, and see
> The saints above, how great their joys,
> How bright their glories be.[3]

From Bunyan's vivid picture of the City and the pilgrims' triumphal entry five pointers may be discerned.

First: mortality is a thing of the past. Pilgrims have left 'their Mortal Garments behind them in the River' and have been 'transfigured', to use Bunyan's apt term, that is, given a new, spiritual form. So then, impurity, injustice and evil have been left behind, as also sorrow, sickness, affliction and death. Time has disappeared. There is no day or night, no ageing, nor fear of tomorrow, for this is the eternal city. Such a conception is beyond our mortal minds, even those of avid science fiction readers. It is for immortal minds.

Secondly, this new life is communal. There is a cross-section of generations, the Communion of Saints. Abraham, Isaac and Jacob are to be found 'resting upon their Beds' alongside recent pilgrims. We are assured that we shall enjoy our friends again. But what are people going to do in heaven? That hoary question Bunyan answers after a thorough search of the Scriptures. We shall walk and talk, even ride; we shall join in praise, even shouting; we shall serve. We shall also have the unenviable responsibility of sitting alongside Christ in judgment at the Second Coming. Life in the eternal city is certainly not all repose. It is not 'an inert immutability', as the theologian Gustaf Aulén remarks. 'Eternal life in terms of mere blessedness and peace' would fail to be 'eternal *life*'.[4]

Thirdly, the community is lively and joyful. For example, when the pilgrims reached the city walls they were met by a heavenly choir singing, 'Blessed are they that are called to the Marriage Feast of the Lamb.' Out came the 'King's Trumpeters, cloathed in white and shining Rayment, who with melodious noises, and loud, made even the Heavens to echo with the sound.' All the bells of the city rang out. The mortal dreamer was not allowed to enter the city but he was able to get a glimpse inside when the gates were opened and he saw that it 'shone like the Sun' and the streets were 'paved with Gold'. Walking about were 'many men with Crowns on their heads, Palms in their hands and golden Harps'. He doesn't say where the women were. Perhaps they were engaged playing their harps instead of idly promenading. Smile if you like at the fanciful imagery, but notice the point being made: the joyfulness of the life.

Fourthly, the heart of the city is God himself. 'Holy, Holy, Holy is the Lord.' This, the cry of the winged creatures of the Jewish Temple, meets the pilgrims as they pass through the gates. God is served continually with praise and thanksgiving but, unlike earthly worship, the Holy One is seen 'as he is' and his 'pleasant voice' is heard. Yet God moves among them and they daily walk and talk 'with the King'.

Fifthly, the citizens of the city all received their training in this world. Return a moment to the inn where Gaius' servant was laying the supper table. Mathew remarked that the sight made his mouth water and Gaius said that 'all Preaching, Books and Ordinances here, are but as the laying of Trenshers, and the setting of Salt upon the Board, when compared with the Feast that our Lord will make for us when we come to his House.'[5] Yet preaching, books and ordinances are but three planks of the bridge between earth and heaven which we call the spiritual life. What about all the rest? Can we not see the whole pilgrimage as preparation, training for a reality which will outstrip what we now call reality?

A last word. However far on the way we have got, we have a duty to share our experience with our fellows, who need encouragement. Ernest Payne, writing about John Bunyan a few years ago, said that modern man knows 'as poignantly as Christian the dilemma of human existence' but 'has no book in his hand' and 'has no faith in Evangelist'.[6] This means that, more than ever before, the work of persuasion falls upon the ordinary Christian pilgrim. Constancy, courage and cheerfulness make one into a living pointer to the Holy City.

1. 1 Peter 1:3.
2. 1 Corinthians 15:20-22.
3. Isaac Watts.
4. *The Faith of the Christian Church,* p 446.
5. PP p 218.
6. *Six Makers of English Religion* (ed G Rupp), p 101.

BRIEF NOTES ON SOME OF THE PERSONS MENTIONED

Augustine, St (354-430) Bishop of Hippo, North Africa. His *Confessions* and *City of God* in particular have been a great influence throughout history.

Bacon, Francis Lord Verulam (1561-1662) Lawyer, statesman and philosopher.

Baden-Powell, Olave, Lady (1889-1977) Wife of Lord Baden-Powell and leader of the world-wide Guide movement.

Baxter, Richard (1615-91) Leading Puritan divine and author; advocate of moderation.

Benedict, St (c480-547) The Father of Western Monasticism. Founded the Benedictines and wrote his Rule at Monte Cassino.

Blake, William (1757-1827) Poet and artist; his *Jerusalem* remains a popular patriotic piece.

Doddridge, Philip (1702-51) Dissenting pastor and Principal of an Academy at Northampton; hymn writer.

Dostoievski, Fedor (1821-81) Russian novelist; author of *Crime and Punishment* and *The Brothers Kazamarov.*

Downame, George (d1634) Bishop of Derry; popular Puritan author.

Francis de Sales (1567-1622) Bishop of Geneva; his writing on spiritual matters has in mind the busy lay person.

Goodall, Norman (1896-1986) URC minister; missionary statesman.

Hammarskjøld, Dag (1905-61) Swedish Secretary-General of UNO. Considered to be an agnostic until his *Markings* was discovered after his death in a plane crash.

Harnack, Adolph (1851-1930) German theologian and Church historian.

Hügel, Friedrich von (1852-1925) Roman Catholic writer on religious and spiritual matters.

Ignatius de Loyola, St (c1491-1556) Spanish soldier and founder of The Society of Jesus.

Jennings, Elizabeth (1926—) Poet with special interest in the relationship of natural and spiritual phenomena.

John of the Cross, St (1542-64) Spanish Carmelite; reformer, mystic and poet; known particularly for his *Dark Night of the Soul.*

Johnson, Samuel (1709-84) Writer, literary critic; famed for his Dictionary.

Julian of Norwich (c1342-1420) Mystic who lived in solitude. There is a joyousness and freshness about her writings.

Kierkegaard, Søren (1813-55) Danish theological writer; protested against the secularisation of the Church.

Lewis, Clive S (1898-1963) Scholar and writer of great wit. His popular *Screwtape Letters* give a devil's-eye view of the Christian life.

Luther, Martin (1483-1546) German, instigator of the Reformation, theologian and translator.

Merton, Thomas (1915-68) American Trappist monk whose work reinvigorated the contemplative life. He was travelling in the East, exploring mysticism, when an accident cut short his life.

Nouwen, Henri American monk and theological teacher who has published several short books on spirituality.

Paton, Alan (1903—) South African, reformer and writer. Well-known for his *Cry the Beloved Country.*

Payne, Ernest (1902-80) Baptist minister, theological teacher and author, ecclesiastical statesman. General Secretary of The Baptist Union of Great Britain and Ireland, 1951-67.

Teresa of Avila, St (1515-82) Spanish Carmelite reformer, who formed the Discalced (barefoot) Carmelites on strict, primitive lines. Famed for mystical experiences. Her *Interior Castle,* concerning prayer, is a classic.

Thomas, Robert S (1913—) Welsh poet, cleric of the Church in Wales.

Watts, Isaac (1674-1748) Congregational divine, educationalist and hymn-writer.

Weil, Simone (1909-43) French philosopher, socialist and writer. Trying to identify with the people of occupied Europe, she starved herself, caught TB and died.

QUESTIONS FOR PERSONAL AND PRIVATE CONSIDERATION AND PRAYER

SETTING OUT

1 What are my goals? Do I tend to drift along?

2 What things do I avoid facing?

3 What about a time of silent meditation? (See *Psalm 62.5*)

4 What is beckoning me on?

5 How much pressure do I put on others?

6 Who is suffering from depression or disappointment? Could I help? Who would help me?

7 How can I tell which person points me in the right way?

INTO TRAINING

8 What were/are my motives in turning to God?

9 Explore the way feelings are expressed with the hands. Offer them to God in prayer.

10 My picture of Jesus – draw or write it down.

11 How have I watered down the fear of God?

12 Do I wrestle in my thinking? Do I wrestle in my praying?

13 Which symbols mean much to you? Thank God.

14 Are there difficult tasks I am putting off?

KNOWING YOURSELF

15 Am I taking sufficient physical exercise and mental relaxation to have a balanced life-style?

16 Am I guilty of cliquishness? Could I broaden my friendships?

17 Which is the weakest part of my spiritual life? How could I remedy this?

18 What about the future? Do I plan for it, pray for it, pray about it, worry about it or ignore it?

19 Do I feel superior — because of class, race, education, life-syle or commitment to Christ?

20 What helps me keep a right estimate of myself? (see *Romans 7.19 and 24*).

21 What have been my worse fears? How were they overcome?

IN COMPANY

22 Make a list of close friends. Give God thanks. How can I show my gratitude to them?

23 Do different parts of my life need reconciling to achieve wholeness?

24 What elements of rebelliousness and bitterness do I find in myself because of the authority others have over me?

25 Do I need to improve my listening skill?

26 What do I talk about but do not do? (see *John 15.1-2*).

27 Who is, or could be, a spiritual counsellor to me? What do I need to be doing about this?

28 Am I sometimes guilty of enjoying 'martyrdom'? When and why?

DARKNESS AND LIGHT

29 In what ways can I use my freedom to help those denied theirs?

30 What excuses do I make instead of obeying God's will?

31 Can I love and not forgive?

32 Can I forgive myself? What makes it possible?

33 When am I rude or annoyed with people?

34 What parts of life do I find easy?

35 What experience of 'the Other' have I for which to give thanks? How did it lead me on?

PASTORAL REFLECTIONS

36 When do I regularly attend to God? What other times and places could I use?

37 What prayers do I make for the ministry in our day?

38 Do people see me as compassionate or patronising? Who needs my compassion now?

39 How can I be a better host?

40 What were my motives for my recent 'good works'?

HOLY WEEK

41 What blessings do I owe to the other sex?

42 How does my leisure help my spiritual life?

43 How much does the Bible influence my life?

44 Am I prepared both to serve and be served?

45 To which events of Good Friday do I need to pay more attention?

46 How does *Pilgrim's Progress* help us to follow Jesus Christ?

47 What makes my idea of the future life full and rich?

QUESTIONS AND ACTIVITIES FOR GROUPS

Groups with experienced leaders will not find it difficult to get discussion going provided that members have read the sections. The simplest way to get the group going would be to ask one member in advance to speak for a few minutes about his or her reactions to the sections and any questions they raised.

However, as a back-up to this and to add variety here are a few further suggestions.

SETTING OUT

A What starts people on the search for answers to life's big questions? What are those questions? How can a modern 'Evangelist' help?

B Have a time of silence (at least 5-10 minutes). Talk about it or write down impressions and then discuss. Do we need silence in worship and in daily life?

C Let members search their Bibles for short passages where disappointment or depression are expressed. A leader may need to help some members by pointing to certain Psalms, to Job, Jeremiah or *John 6.66ff.* Share these together. What evangelical opportunities are there in helping those in trouble and what are the dangers?

INTO TRAINING

D What kind of training does the Church need today for Church Membership? And what kind of in-service training? What are we providing?

E Ask members to bring one or two pictures of Jesus and say what they feel about them. (The leader should bring a reserve number.) What is our mental image of Jesus? Does it, should it change?

F Look at *Acts 3:19, Matthew 15;3, Luke 22:32.* What is meant by conversion?

KNOW YOURSELF

G Suppose you were moving to a completely new place. What would you look for in choosing a church to attend (negatives and positives)? What implications has this for your church life?

H Let each member write down on a piece of paper one weakness in his/her Christian living. Fold the paper a little to hide the word and collect them all and deal out again. Everyone writes down some other weakness. Repeat a few times. Read out the lists and discuss in order of 'merit' (ie. the most often mentioned to the least). Play this game again, this time writing down the weaknesses in other Christians which we find common or annoying or both. Discuss.

I Get each member to find a text or passage in the Bible which has been influential in his/her life. Share them. What parts of Scripture do we find particularly helpful for our prayer life? What would we recommend to a beginner in prayer?

IN COMPANY

J Would one or two in your group try rewriting Faithful's story of his sexual encounters for modern readers? – discuss together.

K Get members to bring along examples from newspapers and magazines etc illustrating the modern Vanity Fair. Where do Christians draw a line?

L What can we learn from Jesus' own words about speaking the truth in love?

DARKNESS AND LIGHT

M What is our church doing for the persecuted? How are we using our freedom? 'We are doing everything we can with the freedom we have, what are you doing with yours?' asked a devout East-European Christian.

N Does forgiveness work? Get members to come along prepared to show instances where it has done and hasn't. Discuss them in the light of the Lord's Prayer.

O Study *II Kings 17.33* in its context. What modern relevance has it?

PASTORAL REFLECTIONS

P What is the difference between being compassionate and soft?

Q Obtain from various people in your church, including the minister, information as to what they most need to further their Christian work and witness. Share the information and discuss what could be done. Pray about it.

R Read in silence and then aloud the story of the cleansing of the Temple. What are its implications for us?

HOLY WEEK

S When you look at the activities of your church under age-ranges, are the energies of the church well distributed among them? What is the way forward?

T How does *Pilgrim's Progress* help us to follow Jesus?

U Read *Hebrews 11.8-16.* Is life a journey or a pilgrimage? What difference does it make?